You're Retired Now.
Relax.

Printed in the United States of America
Library of Congress Catalog Card Number 2007061216
ISBN 978-1-4243-3554-1

For information address:

⊤ **TREASURE COAST** PRESS

4828 N. Kings Hwy. #127 Fort Pierce, FL 34951
TCPbook@aol.com

You're Retired Now. Relax.

BY

MALCOLM D. MAHR

Also by Malcolm D. Mahr

Fiction

Don't Feed Peanuts to a Zombie
The Nude Gioconda

Nonfiction

How to Win in the Yellow Pages
What Makes a Marriage Work

Dedication

This work is dedicated with love and admiration to three very special baby boomers, my sons: Scott, Adam and Jamie.

I've heard that in many cultures, elders summed up their acquired wisdom as the end of their lives approached and passed on these values and lessons. It sounds like a good idea, but I'd rather do it now — on my deathbed I might not be in the mood.

To think that I know all of the answers to retirement living is pure arrogance, but if in the process of reading this book, you or someone you love gains a little more insight about successfully managing the insecurity, the struggle, the fun and the adventure of retirement, then, as they say, this effort will have been worthwhile.

And the last dedication is to my wife, my love, my partner, and my best friend for 56 years, Fran, who proved, for me, that the thing that counted the most in life, in retirement, and in the pursuit of happiness was picking the right companion.

Cartoons

People like to laugh, but there can be a serious side to humor. A good cartoon has three characteristics: a comical truth, a few words, and a fine image.

My thanks to Merrideth Miller of the Cartoon Bank Division of *The New Yorker Magazine* for her patience and cooperation.

Contents

Ten ways to get more out of life.

It ain't over till it's over.
Yogi Berra

Just remember, once you're over the hill
you begin to pick up speed.

Charles Schultz

1

Thou shalt accept what you cannot change – and move on.

Just when the caterpillar thought the world was over, it became a butterfly.

Anonymous

"Mac, your company stock is worth millions. You're rich," said my accountant, Ralph, at posh Marconi's Restaurant in Baltimore.

"Congratulations, we present this award to you as 'Manufacturer of the Year,'" said the president of the Retail Packaging Association in the Caesar's Palace ballroom in Las Vegas.

"Our sales figures are lagging behind forecasts. We need to lower prices to hold on to big customers," said sales manager Lindy.

"Our production costs are higher than expected; we're airfreighting product from the Orient to meet customer delivery demands," said division manager Tom.

"You're hemorrhaging red ink," said accountant Ralph.

"We're tightening your borrowings," said the New York bank that factored our inventory and accounts receivables.

"Try and sell the company," said the board of directors.

"Your white knight has arrived," said lawyer Herb.

"I'll buy you," said wealthy board mill owner Lee. "But we need the bank to be cooperative."

"We can recover all of our borrowings by liquidating you, not by cooperating with new investors," said the bankers.

"Oh my God, we're going bankrupt," said perceptive accounting office clerk Darlene.

"After the liquidation sale, turn in your car and empty your office," said the bankers.

"You're 65, you have no job and your stock is worthless, Mac," said accountant Ralph.

"I love you, we'll get through this," said my precious wife, Fran. "You're retired now. Relax!"

Let go of what you can't change...and move on.
Your attitude is your mental position, mindset, or point of view based on what you believe to be true about life, other people and yourself. Life is never without disappointments, setbacks and problems. The only thing in your power is your attitude toward it. When you take responsibility for your attitude, you can move on.

The only person who welcomes change is a wet baby.

Anonymous

"I thought I'd stay home today and accept the things I can't change."

God grant me the serenity to accept the people I cannot change, the courage to change the one I can, and the wisdom to know...it's me.

John Miller

Change ain't easy.

The woman affectionately known as Dr. Bessie died in 1995 at the age of 104. Bessie Delany was the second black woman licensed to practice dentistry in New York state. In an interview she said, "I thought I could change the world. It took me a hundred years to figure out I can't change the world. I can only change Bessie. And honey, that ain't easy either."

If you don't like something, change it. If you can't change it, change your attitude. Don't complain.

Maya Angelou

Your attitudes influence your behavior.

Dale Carnegie taught that enthusiasm is a learned skill, and if you think you can improve your attitude, you can.

After taking his course, each morning I would look in the bathroom mirror and say, "Act enthusiastic and you'll feel enthusiastic." Then I repeated it louder, "ACT ENTHUSIASTIC AND YOU'LL FEEL ENTHUSIASTIC!"

"WILL YOU PLEASE SHUT UP!" yelled my wife, Fran. "YOU'RE WAKING EVERYBODY UP!.

This uncharacteristic positive behavior will at first startle your family, but it works. And so does the opposite. If you look in the mirror and think your life is in the toilet and you're a loser – guess what – you may be. As ye think, so shall ye be. If you believe everything's going to be all right, it probably will.

My mother said, "You won't amount to anything because you procrastinate." I said, "just wait."

Judy Tenuda

As you think, so shall you be.
You may be surprised to learn that even more than physical health, attitude is one of the best indicators of successful aging. An organization of leading scientists, including three Nobel Laureates, reported at their annual meeting that physical health is not the best indicator of successful aging – attitude is.

The greatest discovery of any generation is that a human being can alter his life by altering his attitude.

William James

Viktor E. Frankl, renowned psychiatrist, died in 1997 at 92. Frankl was author of the landmark book *Man's Search for Meaning* and was one of the world's most important psychiatrists. *Man's Search for Meaning* has sold over 2 million copies and has been translated into 23 languages. The Library of Congress calls the book one of the most influential of the 20th century.

Frankl survived the Holocaust, even though he was in four Nazi death camps from 1942-45. His parents and other members of his family died in the camps.

Life is 10% what happens to me and 90% how I react to it.
Charles R. Swindoll

> *We who lived in concentration camps can remember that everything can be taken from a man but one thing: the last of the human freedoms – to choose one's attitude in any given set of circumstances, to choose one's own way.*
> Viktor E. Frankl

Superman

Christopher Reeve was an American actor, director, producer and writer renowned for his portrayal of Superman in four films from 1978-1987.

In 1995, Reeve was rendered a quadriplegic during an equestrian competition and was confined to a wheelchair for the remainder of his life. The man who played Superman provided an example of how a positive attitude can contribute to an improved physical state.

I think a hero is an ordinary individual who finds strength to persevere and endure in spite of overwhelming obstacles.
Christopher Reeve

Dr. John McDonald is my neighbor and friend. As a key physician for Christopher Reeve, John quotes his patient as saying, "Either you vegetate and look out a window, or activate and try to effect change."

Christopher Reeve became a spokesman for disabled people and a vocal supporter of stem cell research. He died on October 10, 2004, after suffering cardiac arrest.

Be the best of whatever you are.
You may not be ready to leave your family and join the
Peace Corps in Africa or go to Appalachia to build homes
with Habitat for Humanity. But, you *can* be the best of
whatever you are.

Use the talents you possess,
for the woods would be silent
if no birds sang except the best.

Henry van Dyke

> *If you can't be a pine on the top of a hill,*
>   *Be a scrub in the valley – but be*
> *the best little scrub by the side of the hill;*
>   *Be a bush if you can't be a tree.*
> *If you can't be a bush be a bit of the grass*
>   *And some highway happier make,*
> *If you can't be a muskie than just be a bass –*
>   *But the liveliest bass in the lake.*
> *We can't all be captains, we've got to be crew,*
>   *There's something for all of us here.*
> *There's big work to do, and there's lesser to do,*
>   *And the task you must do is the near.*
> *If you can't be a highway then just be a trail,*
>   *If you can't be the sun be a star;*
> *It isn't by size that you win or you fail –*
>   *Be the best of whatever you are.*

Douglas Malloch

2

Have fun while you're living. If not now, when?

Fun is about as good a habit as there is.

Jimmy Buffett

If a man insisted always on being serious, and never allowed himself a bit of fun and relaxation, he would go mad or become unstable without knowing it.

Herodotus

"It's not that we had more fun before we got married — it's just that now we're having a different kind of fun."

Having fun can be good for your health.

The joyful emotions created by play drive our immune and other healing systems in the direction of good health and longevity.

The MacArthur Foundation's study on aging proved that having fun is essential to successful aging. Participating in any of the following activities can provide great pleasure.

Cycling: A good place to start is at your local bike shop where you can try out different models. And they now have soft, cushy seats for which I am posteriorly grateful. Cycling is a good way to get your heart racing without putting too much strain on your joints.

Football: Everybody loves following football, the sport in which twenty-two perfect physical specimens get a three-hour workout combining aerobics and strength training, while fifty million fans who need the exercise sit back and watch them.

If you never did, you should. These things are fun, and fun is good.

Dr. Seuss,
One Fish, Two Fish,
Red Fish, Blue Fish

"Take some identification with you in case you die."

Boating: For the past decade, women have been the fastest-growing segment of the power boating population. On a big birthday, my wife, Fran, paraphrased Dylan Thomas and said, "I will not go quietly into my 60s, I will rage, rage, rage, against the dying of the light – I will buy a boat."

"Are you nuts, Fran? We know nothing about boats."

"How much time do I have left, for God's sake?" she said. "If I don't get a boat now, I'll never get one."

"My answer is NO. And that's final," I announced.

Four months later we had completed our Coast Guard training course and were cruising on the Chesapeake Bay in a used 25-foot Grady White power boat, renamed the *Chez Fran*. "Uh, Mac," she said. "Steering this boat makes me too nervous. Why don't you be the captain?"

"OK, but there can be only one captain on a boat – and that's me. And you have to help with the weekly cleaning."

"Fine, fine," Fran said. "By the way, Muriel is coming to Baltimore to visit us this weekend, and it would be fun to take the boat to Fells Point for breakfast at Jimmie's Restaurant."

Muriel, a White House correspondent, arrived for her boat ride in a black dress and high heeled shoes.

I navigated the craft the short ride to Fells Point. The tide was low. I got close to the high pier, but not near enough to tie up. I didn't know how to make the damn boat go sideways.

People on the pier were laughing and yelling encouragement. "Throw us your lines," they said helpfully.

"Where are your ropes?" I asked Fran.

"My what?" Fran replied.

The way I see it, you got two choices. You either gotta get busy livin'...or get busy dyin.'
Frank Darabout

One helpful soul tossed two lines and pulled us laterally to the pier. With the low tide, we had to climb up four rows of dirty old automobile tires attached as wharf buffers. Muriel, in her stunning black dress and high heels, hauled herself up the side of the pier. The crowd loved it.

That was the final voyage of the *Chez Fran*. Also, Muriel doesn't visit us as much as she used to.

Bowling: According to a recent study, bowling is the most popular fitness sport among Americans. It sounds like fun, but how can it be a fitness sport when you can guzzle beer and eat starchy pizza while you're playing?

Boxing: Boxing is similar to ballet, except there's no music, no choreography, and the dancers hit each other.

> *One of my uncles watches a boxing match and says, "Sure. Ten million dollars. For that kind of money, I'd fight him." As if someone will pay two hundred dollars a ticket to see a fifty-seven-year-old carpet salesman get hit in the face once and cry.*
>
> Larry Miller

Bungee jumping: An activity in which a crazy person jumps off from a high place with one end of an elastic cord attached to his or her body or ankles and the other end tied to the jumping-off point. When the person jumps, the cord will hopefully stretch to take up the energy of the fall. Then the jumper flies upwards as the cord snaps back, oscillating up and down until the initial energy of the jump is dissipated or until the jumper's mother intervenes and whacks the jumper repeatedly with her cane.

One advantage of bowling over golf is that you never lose a bowling ball.

Anonymous

Dance as if no one were watching. Sing as if no one were listening. And live every day as if it were your last.

Anonymous toast

Dancing: Ballroom dancing can be magical and transforming. A 2003 report published in the *New England Journal of Medicine* found that ballroom dancing at least twice a week made people less likely to develop dementia.

Orthopedic surgeons were overjoyed at the news. Many purchased Mercedes as a result of the sudden spurt in hip and knee replacement surgeries.

"Ballroom dancing helps us over our rough spots."

Fishing: I've heard it said that fishing is better than sex, because: It's OK to pay a professional to fish with you, and if your regular fishing partner isn't available, he/she won't object if you fish with someone else. Nobody will ever tell you that you will go blind if you fish by yourself. When dealing with a fishing pro, you never have to wonder if they are really an undercover cop. And, your fishing partner will never say, "Not again? We just fished last week! Is fishing all you ever think about?"

Gardening: Treat yourself to getting dirty without feeling guilty and taking the time to soak up a little peace and serenity.

If people concentrated on the really important things in life, there'd be a shortage of fishing poles.
Doug Larson

A woman's garden is growing beautifully but the darn tomatoes won't ripen. There's a limit to the number of uses for green tomatoes and she's getting tired of waiting. So she goes to her neighbor and says, "Your tomatoes are ripe, mine are green. What can I do about it?"

Her neighbor replies, "Well, it may sound absurd, but here's what to do. Tonight there's no moon. After dark go out into your garden and take all your clothes off. Tomatoes can see in the dark and they'll be embarrassed and blush. In the morning they'll all be red, you'll see."

Well, what the heck? She does it. The next day her neighbor asks how it worked.

"So-so," she answers. "The tomatoes are still green but the cucumbers are all four inches longer."

Gardening is a man's effort to improve his lot.
Anonymous

Golf: In 1923, Who Was:
>One. President of the largest steel company?
>Two. President of the largest gas company?
>Three. President of the New York Stock Exchange?
>Four. Greatest wheat speculator?
>Five. Head of the Bank of International Settlement?
>Six. Great Bear of Wall Street?

These men were considered the world's most successful of their day. In retrospect, 83 years later, what ultimately became of them?

One. The president of the largest steel company, Charles Schwab, died a pauper. Two. The president of the largest gas company, Edward Hopson, went insane. Three. The president of the NYSE, Richard Whitney, was released from prison to die at home. Four. The great wheat speculator, Arthur Cooger, died abroad, penniless. Five. The president of the Bank of International Settlement shot himself. Six. The Great Bear of Wall Street, Cosabee Livermore, also committed suicide.

However, in that same year, the PGA Champion and the winner of the US Open was Gene Sarazen. What became of him?

Sarazen played golf until he was 92 and died at the age of 95. He was financially secure at the time of his death.

The moral: Screw work. Play golf.

Hiking: Oh, to be in the great outdoors, breathing fresh air and traveling up a mountain path on a long, lush hike.

> Two campers are hiking in the woods when one is bitten on the rear end by a deadly rattlesnake. "I'll go and find help," the other says. He runs 10 miles to a small town and finds the town's only doctor, who is busy delivering a baby.
> "I can't leave," the doctor says. "But here's what to do. Take a knife, cut a little 'x' where the bite is, suck out the poison and spit it on the ground."
> The guy runs back to his friend, who is in agony. "What did the doctor say?" the victim asks.
> "He says you're gonna die."

Skiing consists of wearing $3,000 worth of clothes and equipment and driving 200 miles in the snow in order to stand around at a bar and drink.

P. J. O'Rourke

Jogging: My doctor recently told me that jogging could add years to my life. I think he was right. I feel ten years older already.

Skiing: Here's a sport where you can catch cold and go broke while rapidly heading nowhere at great personal risk. The good news is: after your seventieth birthday, you can ski free at many ski resorts, and Medicare will cover most of your hospital costs.

Skydiving: If you're the kind of person that at first you don't succeed, then skydiving definitely isn't for you.

Scuba diving: For people who are great swimmers, not claustrophobic, and not afraid of being mangled by sharks, scuba diving might be just right.

Ever since I started to surf, I realized that golf is for people who don't know how to surf.

Tiger Woods

Surfing: The Hawaiian name for surfing is *he'e nalu*. In ancient times, surfing was a favorite pastime of all the people, but it was the men and women of the *ali'i* (chiefly or royal) class who perfected the riding of waves. To our eldest son, Jamie, Fran wrote *Surfer Man*.

> *Rough seas, surfer man*
> *white foam on the horizon*
> *swells, like too many suds*
> *in the washing machine*
>
> *I watched you leap into the sea*
> *surfer man*
> *your tight body charged*
> *against the incoming tide.*
>
> *Turning at the right moment*
> *to ride the curling wave*
> *into shore, then out again.*
>
> *Defy the shark's fin,*
> *leap with the Dolphin,*
> *feel the warmth of the August Sea.*
> *Be, Be*
> *And I will understand.*

Swimming: Called the "perfect exercise" because you use almost every muscle in your body, swimming is aerobically demanding and stretches you out in a healthy way, like yoga.

For those of you who suffer from back pains, check with your doctor. He or she will probably agree that swimming may be the best way to avoid or relieve back problems.

In my retirement I go for a short swim at least once or twice every day. It's either that or buy a new golf ball.

Gene Perret

There are many good reasons for playing,
One has just entered my head;
If a man doesn't play when he's living,
How the hell can he play when he's dead?

Unknown

Unleash your creativity.

*The question is not whether you are creative enough
but whether you will free yourself to express it.*

Ian Roberts, *Creative Authenticity*

An artist finished painting his nude model, then tried to kiss her. Not fighting him off too fiercely, the model said, "Do you do this with all your models?"

The artist said, "No. You're the first one I ever tried to go to bed with." The model said, "How many models have you had before me?" The artist replied, "Three – an apple, a pear and a banana."

*Question:
"Do you know how old I'll be by the time I learn to paint?"*

*Answer:
"The same age you will be if you don't."*

Do you have a creative bottleneck?

"I'm too old" is one of the things we say to save ourselves from the emotional cost of the ego deflation involved in being a beginner, according to Julia Cameron in *The Artist's Way*. "Often my best students came to their work late. Work begets work. Small actions lead us to the larger movements in our creative lives."

Anna (Grandma Moses) Robertson sold her first paintings to a collector at 79 – and kept at it for the next two decades. I.M. Pei designed Cleveland's Rock and Roll Hall of Fame in his 70s, and Frank Lloyd Wright died at 91 building his final monument, the Guggenheim Museum. Creativity often peaks in our later years. There is no shortage of "late bloomer" role models.

Ten major bottlenecks that creative people commonly face when contemplating a new venture are listed below.

1 ____ "It's too late."
2 ____ "My family and friends will think I'm crazy."
3 ____ "I'm not talented enough."
4 ____ "I'm too busy, but I will do it, one of these days."
5 ____ "I'm not disciplined enough to stick with it."
6 ____ "People may laugh at me."
7 ____ "I can't handle rejection or criticism."
8 ____ "I don't have a conducive place to work."
9 ____ "I don't have money for lessons and equipment."
10 ____ "I'm too old."

Check off any bottleneck that you feel applies to you, then whatever you want to do, just jump in and begin it, fears and all. Action overcomes fear.

Painting: In her 50s, Ray Gesumaria, a female Marine in World War II, a mother of five and a dear friend, started exploring her dormant artistic talent. Starting with crude paint-by-number craft kits, she continued her artistic exploration by enrolling in courses at American University. "At some point," Ray said, "you just have to jump in – fears and all."

Whatever you can do or dream you can, begin it. Boldness has genius, power and magic in it.

Johann Wolfgang von Goethe

Encouraged by instructors, friends and fellow students, she worked hard at her craft. In her sixties, Ray's work received professional recognition and was featured in leading art galleries in the Washington area.

Our precious friend Ray was diagnosed with cancer and died. This gifted lady, with no art background, who started late in life, was able to find the path that unleashed her creativity.

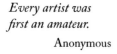

Every artist was first an amateur.
Anonymous

"Woman" – oil, 28 x 22, Ray Gesumaria

In his book *Creative Authenticity*, Ian Roberts insists that ultimately it doesn't matter to the world whether you paint or dance or write. The world will probably get by without the benefit of your creative efforts.

"But that's not the point," says Roberts. "The point is what the inner process of following your creative impulses will do for you. It is about process. Love the work, love the process. Our fascination will pull our attention forward. That, also, will fascinate the viewer."

Book writing: According to *Writer's Digest*, 81 percent of Americans want to write a book, but only 2 percent have completed a manuscript.

Georgia is a friend's daughter who is going through a nasty divorce. "Mr. Mahr, can you help me find a publisher?" she says. "I'm writing about my marital experience."

"Have you completed the manuscript?" I ask.

"I haven't started yet," she replies.

Charles is a graduate of a divinity college, recently arrived from New Orleans. Wearing dreadlocks, earrings and a million-dollar smile, Charles is planning to go to law school. "I have a book in me," he announces. "It's bursting to come out."

"How far have you gotten?" I ask.

"I haven't started it yet," Charles grins, "but it's comin'."

Richard works for the New York State Police. "I really want to write a book," this likable officer says in a serious voice. "Do it," I urge. "Just write a little each day, but start."

With practice comes luck.

Anonymous

If you would be a writer, write.

Anonymous

"I can't right now," Richard says. "With the job and family, I haven't the time. Maybe someday."

Getting started isn't easy. E. L. Doctorow says, "Writing is an exploration. You start from nothing and learn as you go. Writing is like driving at night in the fog. You can only see as far as your headlights, but you can make the whole trip that way."

Barbara Kingsolver won the loyalty of tens of thousands of readers with her novels, *The Bean Trees, Animal Dreams* and *Pigs in Heaven.* To aspiring writers she says, "Close the door. Write with no one looking over your shoulder. Don't try to figure out what other people want to hear from you; figure out what you have to say. It's the one and only thing you have to offer."

Thomas Harris, author of *Silence of the Lambs,* describes his workday. "I get up at 8 o'clock in the morning. At 8:30 am, I leave the house and I arrive at my office at 8:37. I stay in the office until 2 o'clock in the afternoon. I get in my Porsche and I'm home at 2:03 because the one-way streets make it faster for me to drive.

"And between 8:36 am and 2 pm, I'm doing one of three things: I'm writing. I'm staring out the window. Or I'm writhing on the floor."

Many people hear voices when no one is there. Some of them are called mad and are shut up in rooms where they stare at the walls all day. Others are called writers and they do pretty much the same thing.
Meg Chittenden

Writing is like prostitution. First you do it for love, and then for a few close friends, and then for money.
Moliere

When I was 65, my company went into bankruptcy; I was out of a job. After taking a course in advertising, I became a consultant to help advertisers improve their ads, reduce their costs, and protect them from the descending hordes of aggressive Yellow Pages sales reps.

At age 71, I wrote a book, *How to Win in the Yellow Pages*, which received an award from *Writer's Digest* and a five star rating on Amazon.com.

A few years later, what started out as a gift for friends and family on Fran's and my fiftieth wedding anniversary, *What Makes a Marriage Work*, was contracted for and published by Durban House Publishing.

One Sunday afternoon at Borders bookstore in Stuart, Florida, I was well-positioned at the store's mall opening with books stacked up ready for a book signing. People entering Borders eyed me warily, like if they got too close and touched me, they would contact leprosy – or worse – have to spend money. A little girl of 12 asked, "How much does the book cost?"

"Fourteen ninety-five, dear," I said. "Why, are you interested in buying one for your mother?"

"No," she replied, "I want to get it for a friend."

"How old is your friend?"

"She's thirteen."

"This is a book about marriage. Your friend's a tad young, but thank you for stopping by."

The store manager wandered over to see how things were going. I told him about the cute little girl. "You should have taken her money," he said. "A sale's a sale."

An elderly woman stopped by, scanned the book and laughed at the *New Yorker* cartoons.

"I'd be happy to sign a copy for you," I said.

"I just got money for my last novel."
"Which publisher?"
"No publisher. UPS – they lost it."
Anonymous

She was joined by a baldheaded, barrel-chested guy who glared at me, grabbed the woman's arm and snarled, "We don't need no goddamn help with our goddamn marriage."

A dozen books were sold, but the long afternoon was wearing me down. At three o'clock, as scheduled, I started to pack up in preparation for leaving. *I'm 76 years old. Why am I doing this?* I wondered. *It's a beautiful day. My friends are out on the golf course. I'm sitting here dressed in a tie and jacket hawking my books. It cost more for lunch and gas than I made in book royalties today. This is ridiculous. Get a life, Mac!*

As I was getting ready to leave, an attractive blonde, who had purchased a book two hours earlier, rushed up breathlessly.

"I'm so glad I caught you before you left," she said.

Oh, great! I thought. *She wants to return her book.*

The blonde said, "I was reading *What Makes a Marriage Work* while I was sitting in the beauty parlor, and I had to come back and tell you how much I loved it. Thank you so much!"

AHHHHH! The recognition of our creative efforts, particularly from pretty blondes, makes it all worthwhile. And it's never too late!

Writing is the hardest way of earning a living, with the possible exception of wrestling alligators.

Olin Miller

*I merely took the
energy it takes to pout
and wrote some blues.*

Duke Ellington

Songwriting: "Songwriting," says Paul McCartney, "is like psychiatry. You sit down and dredge up something deep inside and bring it out front."

Free songwriting courses are available online. Try the step-by-step approach offered at **www.easy-song writing. com.**

*"This next one is a hard-rockin', kick-ass, take-no-prisoners
tune we wrote about turning sixty."*

Photography: Photography is one of the fastest-growing hobbies in the world. Digital cameras now make it possible for anyone with a little imagination and a steady hand to produce exciting pictures and get prints or e-mail them worldwide.

Poetry: In the mid-1970s Fran was writing poetry. She was published in a volume of poetry entitled *Rye Bread: Women Poets Rising*. She asked if I minded if she went off on a poetry weekend.

"What's a poetry weekend?"

"Well," she said, "a group of men and women from my poetry class at Towson State are going to Ocean City (Maryland) to write and critique poetry and stuff like that." Upon her return Sunday night, Fran seemed euphoric.

"We walked in the snow," she related. "And we sat by the fire, held hands, drank cheap wine, discussed poetry, and everyone had an incredible experience."

"Did you find time for writing?" I asked sarcastically.

"Here's one I wrote," Fran said.

> *You are the sea*
> *you covet me*
> *Your tide washes away*
> *my loneliness*
> *Without you I am a shell*
> *drifting weightless*
> *in a North Wind.*

"Wow!" I said, "what a terrific poem. And to think, you wrote this poem especially for me...it is me coveting you and washing away your loneliness, isn't it? Fran? FRAN?"

Painting is silent poetry, and poetry is painting that speaks.
Plutarch

Work begets work. There is no other way.

It is a myth to believe creativity is the property of a few gifted individuals. Everyone has creative potential. The big question is not whether you are creative enough but whether you will free yourself to express it. We learn by practicing our craft and thereby gain experience. Work begets work. There is no other way.

Whatever you want to do creatively, just jump in and do it, fears and all. Action overcomes fear. Yes, yes, yes.

Never let the fear of striking out get in your way.
Babe Ruth

> *But why, you ask me, should this tale be told*
> *To men grown old, or who are growing old?*
> *It is too late! Ah, nothing is too late*
> *Till the tired heart shall cease to palpitate.*
> *Chaucer, at Woodstock with the nightingales,*
> *At sixty wrote the Canterbury Tales;*
> *Goethe at Weimar, toiling to the last,*
> *Completed Faust when eighty years were past.*
>
> *What then? Shall we sit idly down and say*
> *The night hath come; it is no longer day?*
> *Even the oldest tree some fruit may bear;*
> *For age is opportunity no less*
> *Than youth itself, though in another dress,*
> *And as the evening twilight fades away*
> *The sky is filled with stars, invisible by day.*
>
> Henry Wadsworth Longfellow,
> *Morituri Salutamus*

Explore, Dream, Discover.

Don't wait until it's too late to travel. Explore, dream, and discover while you can.

"Twenty years from now," Mark Twain said, "you will be more disappointed by the things that you didn't do than by the ones you did do. So throw off the bowlines. Sail away from the safe harbor. Catch the trade winds in your sails. Explore. Dream. Discover."

Though we travel the world over to find the beautiful, we must carry it with us or we find it not.

Ralph Waldo Emerson

"Can you suggest some place where the dollar goes far but they don't want to kill us?"

l'incidente dell'automobile: Arriving at Milano's Malpensa Airport, we picked up a new, factory-fresh, standard shift, leased Peugeot. Fran did the driving, because I only drive automatic shift.

I thought we would easily locate the hotel that travel writer Rick Steves recommended near the Duomo. However, Milano's central city is a labyrinth of intersecting streets. When we arrived at the hotel, Fran edged the new Peugeot near the entrance, not noticing the two-foot-high stone pylons lining the street. BANG! went the Peugeot's crumpled left front fender.

The Speranari was a small, friendly, economy hotel with no frills or helpful doormen. I struggled with the heavy luggage – sweating and gasping for air – up the steep, narrow flight to the lobby and said to Fran, "You get settled in while I park the car."

"You don't drive standard shift," she protested.

"Not to worry," I answered.

I grappled with the unfamiliar gear shift and was swept away in the busy end-of-day traffic. Confused, I mistakenly entered a one-way street, and while backing up, I hit a pylon, CRASH! smashing the right rear fender.

My frustration mixed with panic. I shoved the gear shift aggressively. Gray smoke spewed from under the hood. A noxious burning-plastic smell was detectable.

Driving in front of me was a police car. To attract attention, I pressed hard on the horn. The police car came to a screeching halt. Two large *carabiniere* stepped out, dressed in elegant blue and purple uniforms decorated with gold epaulets and tassels.

Life is not measured by the number of breaths we take, but by the places and moments that take our breath away.

Anonymous

One officer ambled over to my car, pressed his fingers to his nose, pointed to the engine and said, "*Kaput.*"

"Do you speak English? I'm old and lost," I said.

"Eh?" he responded.

"*Dové la Piazza Duomo?*" I stammered.

"*Allora,*" he said, motioning that I should follow their car. Twenty minutes later the Peugeot was parked in the Duomo self service parking area, smoke still seeping from under the hood. The acrid odor was pervasive.

"WHERE WERE YOU?" Fran said. "I was so upset I called Scott in New York and told him you were lost in Milano."

"What did Scott say?"

"He said he could leave his job, catch a cab to Kennedy, spend whatever it cost to fly to Milano and sit with me until your dead body showed up. Or, I could watch CNN until you got back."

"Excuse me, dear, I have to make an important call."

Taking out a card from my wallet, I dialed the number. "Hello. Peugeot?" I said, "There's something wrong with the leased car I picked up today at Malpensa Airport. It has a funny smell – like maybe there's something wrong with the transmission.

"You want me to drive the car to your garage? NO WAY! I'm afraid that neither the car nor I can manage that.

"WHAT? You say you're going to send a taxi to take me to Hertz for a loaner car – at no cost. GRAZIE!"

"You had all the excitement," Fran said, "while I had to stay here cooped up in the room. Some fun trip!"

Explore America: There are unforgettable places to visit driving cross country from Alaska's Inside Passage to Savannah's Historic District, to the French Quarter in New Orleans, the Las Vegas Strip to New York's Finger Lakes Region, Monticello in Virginia to Jackson Hole in Wyoming, to eating steamed crabs in Baltimore.

We may run, walk, stumble, drive, or fly, but let us never lose sight of the reason for the journey, or miss a chance to see a rainbow on the way.

Anonymous

"O.K., this is the West Coast, O.K.? What you want is the East Coast, so turn around and go back twenty-four, twenty-five hundred miles, and that's the East Coast. You can't miss it."

S.S. ALL YOU CAN EAT

Man cannot discover new oceans unless he has courage to lose sight of the shore.

Andre Gide

Have a cruise adventure: Head for the high seas and the excitement of a cruise! Choose from a long list of exotic destinations. Explore fascinating ports, and enjoy all the fun-filled activities on board your oceanliner.

At **Cruisemates.com**, 99 travel agencies compete to give you the best prices for the dates you specify in advance. CruiseMates is not a travel agency. *The New York Times* said, "Many sites that offer reviews are selling cruises, which raises questions about impartiality. An exception is CruiseMates."

You can find which cruise ships are the best for families, best for singles, best for nightlife, and best for cuisine.

Discover offbeat things to see: When you think of museums, what comes to mind? The Getty in Los Angeles? The Visionary Art Museum in Baltimore? The Guggenheim or MOMA in New York? Yes, those will always draw a crowd, but offbeat museums are popping up.

If you come to a fork in the road – take it.
Yogi Berra

* UFO Sightings: International UFO Museum & Research Center, Roswell, N.M. The exhibits include information about extraterrestrial life forms. The museum endeavors to present facts and be taken seriously, but is undermined by the circus atmosphere that pervades Roswell.

* Cockroaches: The Cockroach Hall of Fame is in Plano, Texas. This small museum features costumed roaches such as a spike-heeled, blonde-wigged Marilyn Monroach and a rhinestone-studded Liberoachi.

* G-Strings: The Burlesque Hall of Fame Museum contains provocative artifacts: sexy photos, G-strings, costumes, fans, boas, and other show-stopping accouterments of the "women of classic burlesque theater" that make for an eye-popping tour in Helendale, California.

* Rattlesnakes: The American International Rattlesnake Museum in Albuquerque, New Mexico, is the largest collection of live rattlesnakes in the world.

A guy was driving down a lonely New Mexico country road one cold winter day when it began to sleet pretty heavily. His windows were getting icy and the wiper blades were badly worn and quickly fell apart under the strain.

Unable to drive any further because of the ice building up on his front window, the man suddenly had a great idea. He stopped and began to overturn large rocks until he located two very lethargic hibernating rattlesnakes.

The man grabbed them up, straightened them out flat and installed them on his blades and they worked just fine.

You've never heard of wind-chilled-vipers?

Elderhostel: Elderhostel is the world's largest education and travel organization for adults fifty-five and over. Each year Elderhostel draws more than 300,000 people to their 1,900 U.S., Canadian and international locations. Elderhostel combines travel with education at very reasonable cost. **www.elderhostel.org**

The journey is the reward.
Taoist proverb

If I had my life to live over, I would take more trips, pick more daisies, climb more mountains, swim more rivers, and watch more sunsets. I've had my moments, and if I had it to do all over again, I'd try to have nothing else, just moments, one after the other.
Nadine Star (at age 89)

Unusual travel signage: Here are some humorous signs and notices written in English that were discovered by Danny Wildner.

In a Bucharest hotel lobby:
> "The lift is being fixed for the next day. During that time we regret that you will be unbearable."

In a Japanese hotel:
> "You are invited to take advantage of the chambermaid."

On the menu of a Swiss restaurant:
> "Our wines leave you nothing to hope for."

In a Bangkok dry cleaner's:
> "Drop your trousers here for best results."

Outside a Paris dress shop:
> "Dresses for street walking."

In a Rhodes tailor shop:
> "Order your summers suits. Because is big rush we will execute customers in strict rotation."

In a Zurich hotel:
> "Because of the impropriety of entertaining guests of the opposite sex in the bedroom, it is suggested that the lobby be used for this purpose."

If you reject the food, ignore the customs, fear the religion and avoid the people, you might better stay home.

James Michener

In an advertisement by a Hong Kong dentist:
"Teeth extracted by the latest Methodists."

In a Rome laundry:
"Ladies, leave your clothes here and spend the afternoon having a good time."

In a Swiss mountain inn:
"Special today – no ice cream."

In a Bangkok temple:
"It is forbidden to enter a woman even a foreigner if dressed as a man."

In a Copenhagen airline ticket office:
"We take your bags and send them in all directions."

A journey of a thousand miles begins with a cash advance.

Anonymous

In a Norwegian cocktail lounge:
"Ladies are requested not to have children in the bar."

In an Acapulco hotel:
"The manager has personally passed all the water served here."

3   Exercise as if your life depends on it – it does.

In twenty years failure to exercise six days a week will seem as self-destructive as smoking two packs of cigarettes a day.

Henry S. Lodge, MD, *Younger Next Year*

"Harry, take it from me. You're doing yourself more harm than good."

He who has health has hope, and he who has hope has everything.

Arabian proverb

Warning: Not Exercising is Hazardous to Your Health!

Take care of your body. It's the only place you have to live. It's never too late to get started. The German proverb *Rast ich, so rost ich* (When I rest, I rust) doesn't apply to just the elderly. Regular exercise, especially activity that includes aerobic exercise and strength training with weights, offers a wide range of benefits to people of all ages.

According to the Surgeon General's report, you need to burn at least two thousand calories a week to begin reaping the benefits of physical activity. How does one measure two thousand calories? Translation into time: that's thirty minutes of physical activity a day, six days a week.

Your body craves the daily chemistry of exercise. Whether the exercise is walking, running, swimming, or using the exercise machines at the gym, what's important is the dailyness of it, six days a week. Carve out the time to exercise, make it protected time and guard it fiercely against intrusion.

The Gym

Health nuts are going to feel stupid someday, lying in hospitals dying of nothing.

Redd Foxx

My legs were getting creakier and my back ached, so I decided to start exercising regularly at a gym.

"Are you looking for the dry cleaners, old timer?" said Frank, the owner of the Fort Pierce, Florida, gym. "It's next door."

"No. I read that it's never too late to exercise," I said. "What can you do to help me get fit?"

"How old are you and how will you pay?" he asked.

"Seventy-eight and Visa," I answered.

"Start slow – you don't want to overdo it," Frank

advised. "We'll begin with a light workout program and see how it goes."

Turning to a pretty Nordic-looking assistant, Frank said, "Shaina, let him warm up for six minutes on the inclined bicycle."

"Don't overdo it," Shaina repeated the caution. Under my workout trunks I was wearing cotton boxer underwear. As I started pedaling on the inclined bike, gravity and the circular leg motion caused my trunks and underwear to ride high up my thighs. I tugged on my shorts – trying not to appear conspicuous.

Tugging didn't work. The cool, circulating air of the gym whirled around my semi-exposed testicles. The woman on the adjoining inclined bike eyed me with suspicion. I visualized the police hauling me off in handcuffs, charged with indecent exposure. Embarrassed and unable to correct my wardrobe malfunction, I stopped pedaling.

Pretty Shaina rushed over. "ARE YOU OKAY, MAC?"

"Everything's fine," I lied. "I wanted to start slowly and not overdo it the first time."

Shaina conducted a hushed conversation with the owner. Frank shot me a worried look. He didn't want people keeling over dead in his health club. It wouldn't be good for business.

Shaina reduced my first-day workout program to minimum weights on six machines. As I was leaving, Frank appeared relieved.

"How soon do you go back north?" he asked.

I don't exercise. If God had wanted me to bend over, he would have put diamonds on the floor.
    Joan Rivers

Start slowly—don't overdo it.

A common mistake, particularly with weight training, is exercising too hard when you start with an exercise program only to get exhausted, injured, or discouraged. Here are a few exercises you can do at home.

Begin with a five-pound potato sack in each hand; extend your arms straight out to your sides and hold them there as long as you can.

After a few weeks, move up to 10-pound potato sacks, then 50-pound potato sacks, and finally you will get to where you will be able to lift a 100-pound potato sack in each hand and hold your arms straight out for more than a full minute!

Next, you put a few potatoes in the sacks, but I would caution you not to overdo it at this level.

Physical activity may be the "magic bullet."

"Exercising is the closest thing to a 'magic bullet,' to ensure longevity and a good quality of life," says Colin Milner, CEO of the International Council on Active Aging.

Ten years of groundbreaking research went into the MacArthur Foundation study on aging in America. The study proved beyond doubt that physical activity cuts the rate of coronary heart disease. The more physical activity you participate in, the lower your risk. Couch potatoes are 80 percent more likely to develop coronary disease than active people. Exercise also cuts the risk of getting hypertension 50 percent, and helps lower existing high blood pressure.

If it weren't for the fact that the TV set and the refrigerator are so far apart, some of us wouldn't get any exercise at all.
Joey Adams

A study published in the May 2005 issue of *Journal of the American Medical Association* finds women with breast cancer who exercised lived longer than those who did not. Survival improved by 50 percent for women who walked the equivalent of three to five hours a week.

Nothing lifts me out of a bad mood better than a hard workout on my treadmill. It never fails. Exercise is nothing short of a miracle.

Cher

Reduce arthritis pain by 50 percent—or more.
Six months ago, I couldn't get out of bed in the morning without back pain. I couldn't sit in a comfortable chair and read without feeling an electric current throbbing in my upper shoulder. I had difficulty sitting at the computer and writing. I talked to my doctor and made an appointment with a top Hopkins back specialist.

"You have osteoarthritis," the doctor said. He gave me a prescription for 800 mg of ibuprofen and recommended physical therapy and weight loss. I didn't take the ibuprofen. Instead, I started stretching, swimming six days a week and cut down on my intake of unhealthy starches – the white stuff.

Before I swim, I do a back stretching exercise that an ex-boxer taught me years ago at the YMCA. I stand with my back flat against a wall, feet 12 inches in front. I stretch my hands high over my head ten times. The swimming and stretching has worked and 75 percent of my back problems have disappeared.

Osteoarthritis is by far the most common type of arthritis, and the percentage of people who have it grows higher with age. An estimated 12.1 percent of the U.S. population (nearly 21 million Americans) age 25 and older have osteoarthritis.

It was funny when comedian Jack Benny said, "I don't deserve this award, but I have arthritis and I don't deserve that either." But, as the population ages, the number of people with osteoarthritis will also grow. By 2030, 20 percent of Americans – about 72 million people– will have passed their 65th birthday and will be at high risk for the disease. And that ain't funny.

The doctor called Mrs. Cohen saying "Mrs Cohen, your check came back." Mrs. Cohen answered "So did my arthritis!"

Henny Youngman

Aerobic exercises

Any physical movement burns calories, but the exercise that uses the most energy is aerobic. The word "aerobic" comes from the Greek word meaning "with oxygen." Jogging, brisk walking, swimming, cross-country skiing, aerobic dancing, and biking are some popular forms of aerobic exercise.

The word 'aerobics' really came about when the gym instructors got together and said: If we're going to charge $10 an hour, we can't call it jumping up and down.

Rita Rudner

Weight training

Both aerobic exercise and weight training offer important benefits to older people. Aerobic exercise is primarily about your muscles' ability to endure. Weight or strength training is about your muscles' ability to deliver power. The MacArthur Foundation study on aging in America reported, "Contrary to popular belief, we now know that pumping iron can help you lose weight."

"Weight training is also good for people with arthritis," says Dr. Henry Lodge in *Younger Next Year*. "Most arthritis patients report a 50 percent reduction in pain and limitation within several months of strength training; minor arthritis usually disappears entirely."

Lodge cautions, "If you have significant arthritis, talk to your doctor about having a physical therapist guide you in the initial stages of your weight-training program."

Most weightlifters are biceptual.

John Rostoni

Those who think they have no time for bodily exercise will sooner or later have to find time for illness.

Edward Stanley

Use exercise to combat depression.

One of the main advantages of using exercise to boost your mood is that the effect is instant. Antidepressants usually take between two and three weeks to kick in, which can be a long time if you're feeling really blue.

Study after study shows that exercise combats depression. It can lift your mood, restore your energy, and a brisk 30-minute walk or jog three times a week may be just as effective in relieving major depression as are standard antidepressant drugs.

A vigorous five-mile walk will do more good for an unhappy but otherwise healthy adult than all the medicine and psychology in the world.

Dr. Paul Dudley White

Exercise your mind.

Keep learning new things and pursuing activities that are mentally stimulating. Never let the brain idle. An idle mind is the devil's workshop. And the devil's name is Alzheimer's.

Unknown

"Hi. I'm, I'm, I'm ... You'll have to forgive me, I'm terrible with names."

Just as physical activity keeps your body strong, mental activity keeps your mind sharp and agile. One way to do this is to challenge yourself by learning new skills. If you continue to learn and challenge yourself, your brain continues to grow, literally. An active brain produces new connections between nerve cells that allow cells to communicate with one another. This helps your brain store and retrieve information more easily, regardless of age.

How many times have you walked into a room and forgotten what you came for? Or acquaintances' names are harder to remember? Such moments of forgetfulness happen to everyone, even young people, but as we get older we wonder, what's going on? And we worry, is this the beginning of Alzheimer's disease, the progressive dementia that now affects 4 million Americans?

I have trouble remembering three things: faces, names, and – I can't remember what the third is.

Fred Allen

Memory is linked to associations.
When we are younger, the brain subconsciously links a name through a sensory association. As we age, the brain seems to lose cells in areas that produce important neurotransmitters, upsetting the brain's delicate balance of these chemical messengers.

One elderly couple is visiting another for supper. The two women go into the kitchen for a moment, leaving the men to talk. One of the men says to the other, "The Mrs. and I went to the nicest restaurant last night."

"Is that so?" the host asks. "What was it called?"

"I can't remember," his guest replies. "Let me think. What's the name of that red flower with thorns all over it?"

"A rose?" the host responds.

"YEAH, THAT'S IT!" he says, then whirls around and yells into the kitchen, "Hey, Rose! What was the name of that restaurant we went to last night!?"

We can improve our short-term memory by utilizing the following association techniques.

Associate by using visual images: The more outlandish the better. If you want to be able to recall someone's name after you first hear it, think of a visual image.

If someone's name is George, imagine him with a white wig cutting down a cherry tree. Let your imagination soar. For Cindy see Cinderella stepping out of a carriage at midnight. For Alice, have her crawling down the rabbit hole in Alice in Wonderland; for Adam envision a man wearing a fig leaf in the Garden of Eden; for every name invent a colorful association.

Let's try a visual association exercise. Pick four first names; create a distinctive visual image for each one and write them down.

Name   Visual image

_____

_____

_____

_____

(Now. Close your eyes and repeat the four names.)

*Cogito ergo sum
(I think; therefore I yam.)*
Anonymous

Associate using rhyming cues: Fifty years ago, in a Dale Carnegie course, I was taught how to remember a list of ten things. Over the years, whether it was a shopping list, a speech, or planning a packaging presentation for my company's major customers like J. C. Penney, The Limited Stores, Corning Glass, Belks or Saks Fifth Avenue, I found this rhyming technique invaluable.

The fact that I still use this handy association cue list today is a testimony to its effectiveness. To increase your ability to associate and remember things, memorize this list of cues.

One.......Run
Two......Zoo
Three....Tree
Four......Door
Five...... Hive
Six.........Sex
Seven....Heaven
Eight......Gate
Nine......Wine
Ten........Den

Exercise zee little gray cells.
Hercule Poirot

EXAMPLE: The morning I was writing this chapter, I woke up knowing I had three important things to remember to do: to contact my editor, Bob, who lives in Vienna, Virginia; to go to the library to get a resource book; and to ask a writer friend, Muriel, to proofread six chapters.

I visualized:

One / Run: I pictured lanky, six-foot-three Editor Bob running stark naked down the main street in Vienna, Virginia. (Not a pretty sight – sorry, Bob.)

Two / Zoo: I visualized a zoo cage full of screeching monkeys reading library books.

Three / Tree: I visualized Muriel sleeping in a hammock slung between two trees – snoring loudly.

Old minds are like old horses; you must exercise them if you wish to keep them in working order.

Anonymous

This association technique works. It really does! Try reciting the rhyming list, then write any ten things you would like to buy, or do, or see, or need or whatever.

One_____

Two_____

Three_____

Four_____

Five_____

Six_____

Seven_____

Eight_____

Nine_____

Ten_____

(Now. Close your eyes, recite the ten rhyming cues and see how many on your list you can remember.)

Eight ways to keep your mind sharp.

1 *Play Scrabble or do crossword puzzles*: Doing crossword puzzles cuts the risk of Alzheimer's 38 percent. Recent studies in the *Journal of the American Medical Association* show that there's no better way to relax, recharge, and reenergize your brain than by solving a crossword puzzle. So why wait? Pick up a pencil and give your cerebral muscles an enjoyable workout.

Iron rusts from disuse, stagnant water loses its purity and in cold weather becomes frozen; even so does inaction sap the vigors of the mind.
Leonardo da Vinci

2 *Learn a foreign language*: Learning a foreign language will make your travels more fun. In 1978, Fran and I went to Spain. In preparation for the trip I signed up for a Spanish refresher class. Fran attended the first session, complained of a headache and dropped out of the course.

We flew to Torremolinos, a Spanish resort on the Costa del Sol. Going out on the sandy beach, I spotted an umbrella-beach chair concessionaire and waved him over.

"*Quanta costa, Señor,*" I asked.

"*Cincocientosdólaresparalasillayelparaguas.*"

I smiled and asked him to speak a little slower. "*Habla mucho despacio, por favor, Señor,*" I said.

The umbrella man frowned and repeated slowly, "*Cincocientosdólaresparalasillayelparaguas.*"

"Why's it taking so long for chairs?" Fran asked.

"I don't know what the hell the guy's saying."

Fran called out, "Hey." She pointed to the chairs and umbrella, hunched her shoulders and opened her palms.

Umbrellaman grinned and held up five fingers.

Fran shook her head and held up two fingers.

Grumbling, the concessionaire lifted three fingers.

"You and your Spanish lessons. Give the man three

hundred pesos and let's get some sun, for God's sake."

I handed him the money. "*Gracias, amigo*," I said.

"No problem, pal," he replied.

4 *Learn to play a musical instrument*: You will never lose the skills you learn (they'll get a bit rusty if you don't use them, but they'll come back when needed - like riding a bike.)

Many people get great pleasure from playing musical instruments at home. These days you can choose from literally thousands of karaoke songs on CDs to accompany your playing.

Music washes away from the soul the dust of everyday life.

Berthold Auerbach

"Play 'Misty' for me."

5 *Learn to operate a computer*: Online communication is bringing generations closer together. The ability to receive an e-mail with pictures of a grandchild or family member living across the street or halfway around the world has impacted life in a profound way.

And once seniors overcome the initial resistance to new technology, they tend to use the Internet even more avidly than younger people to track investments, touch base with friends, look up new recipes, play cards, check the weather, and come across all kinds of interesting things.

"Oh baby . . . oh baby . . . oh baby . . ."

6 *Interact with others*: "Just keeping busy tunes the brain," says Yaakov Stern of Columbia University College of Physicians and Surgeons. Stern followed 1,800 older adults for up to seven years. The more they interacted with others – even just visiting friends, playing cards or going to movies – the lower their risk of developing Alzheimer's.

7 *Be a college "drop-in"*: Go back to school! Take classes, attend lectures in arts, history, music, or almost anything. Learn online. Go to **http://vu.org**. Virtual University is the world's largest online learning community, serving 500,000 students and alumni in 128 countries.

8 *Stretch your mental muscles...read*: Walt Whitman said, "Reading is not a half-sleep, but in the highest sense, an exercise, a gymnast's struggle; in that the reader has to do something for himself. A good book, like healthy exercise, can give you a pleasant sense of fatigue that comes from having stretched your mental muscles."

Why read when you can download 5,000 songs on an iPod or watch TV six hours per day—which is the national average? The typical American retiree watches 26 hours of TV each week, and takes advantage of few, if any, learning opportunities.

"Research indicates that watching television literally numbs the brain," says Lawrence Katz, a professor of neurology at Duke University Medical Center. "The brain is less active during TV-viewing than during sleep!" Katz adds, "And a constant diet of television is linked to fewer social interactions, which in turn has long-term negative consequences."

The brain is unique in that it is the only container of which can be said that the more you put into it, the more it will hold.

Glen Doman

The best brain sharpener may be...exercise.
"Walking 45 minutes three times a week for six months significantly improves mental ability of older adults with no dementia," says Arthur Kramer, a psychologist at the University of Illinois. For older people in particular, even a moderate program of exercise can boost brain health and cognition.

Physical exercise is good for your heart and also good for your brain. So turn off the TV and go for a walk. You'll live longer – and you'll stay sharper too.

The nuclear generator of brain sludge is television.
Dave Barry

You have brains in your head.
You have feet in your shoes.
You can steer yourself
any direction you choose.
Dr. Seuss,
Oh The Places You'll Go!

4

Forgo fad diets and quit eating starchy foods.

The number that stares up at you from your bathroom scale is the most important measure of your future health.

Walter C. Willet, MD, *Eat, Drink, and Be Healthy*

If I can do it, anybody can.

The meaning of the word "diet" has been twisted around. "Diet" comes from the Latin *diaeta*, which means "a way of life." I was seeking a sensible eating "way of life" that would be healthy, nutritious, and would help me lose weight and keep it off.

I kept trying to lose weight...but it kept finding me. In my early teens, my mother took me to a store in Baltimore, Hutzlers, because they had a section called "Huskies." To call it "Pants for fatties" would have been less inviting. At fourteen I went to Staunton Military Academy, where the fat was melted off in sports and exercise, and in 1952, I returned from the Korean War weighing a scrawny 150 pounds.

For years I battled the bulge with jogging and tennis. In my 60s, calcium deposits on the knees eliminated jogging; in my 70s, pulled hamstring muscles caused doctors to advise me to quit tennis and take up golf. Driving around in a golf cart isn't exactly aerobic exercise, and my weight problems returned. I had to start taking Diovan for blood pressure and Zetia for cholesterol.

A waist is a terrible thing to mind.

Tom Wilson

In 2006 doctors found a melanoma cancer on my arm from too much sun exposure. It was operated on and successfully removed. For a while I couldn't exercise, and feeling sorry for myself, I ate whatever I thought would make me feel good. As my weight ballooned to 200 pounds, the arthritis in my back became noticeably more painful. The last straw was trying to wear my tuxedo to a wedding holding the pants together with a large safety pin, hidden by my cummerbund. All evening I was afraid the pin would come loose and perforate my abdomen.

I'm convinced most people only take weight loss seriously if they suffer from either physical pain or social embarrassment— or in my case, both. My weight is now 179, and according to the BMI or Body Mass Index table, that's about right. If I can do it, anybody can.

Let's get real. Fad diets fail because of diets' worst enemies – deprivation and boredom. In her book *French Women Don't Get Fat*, Mirielle Guiliano said, "Deprivation is the mother of failure. Any program that your mind interprets as punishment is one your mind is bound to rebel against. Months of hard-core dieting might well be enough to crush anyone's spirit."

The No-Diet Diet.

1 *Exercise six days a week.* It may be a scientific fact or an old wives' tale, but if you do something 17 days in a row, it will become a habit. I chose swimming, and now it is second nature to head to the pool every morning.

2 *Quit eating starch – the white foods.* I didn't want to feel hungry or bored with the food I ate. I knew if I felt virtuous but deprived, no eating program would last. So *all* I did was quit eating starchy foods – the refined carbohydrates.

I avoid the bad carbs: the white foods like bread, potatoes, white rice. Something strange happens. As I eliminate starches, I no longer have the urgent craving for sweets.

When I want something tasty at night, I take one of the good carbs – fruit. Not only can an apple a day keep the doctor away, but it can also ease arthritis because apples contain boron, a mineral that is helpful in reducing the risk of osteoarthritis.

So, if you want to lose a pound a week, start exercising six days a week and quit eating starchy bread and potatoes. And did you know that one can of soda per day at 150 calories equals a fifteen-pound weight gain per year? Drink water instead of soda.

That's the dirty little secret of my No-Diet Diet.

Drink plenty of water.
In normal weather, you lose about four pints of water a day through urinating, sweating and exhaling. In hot weather, dry climates, or with increased exercise or activity, you lose more.

As we age, our body fluid thirst-indicators often fail to operate, and older people can become dehydrated without realizing it. Drinking plenty of water is beneficial to the immune system, and good hydration reduces the risk of kidney stones.

The U.S. National Research Council recommends that if you eat a 2000-calorie-a-day diet, you need two quarts of water (there's your eight-glass-a-day rule).

Obesity is really widespread.
Joseph O. Keron II

"I still manage to find the time to drink eight glasses of water a day."

The final word on nutrition and health.

Here's the final word on nutrition and health. It's a relief to know the truth after many conflicting medical studies.

The Japanese eat very little fat and suffer fewer heart attacks than the British or Americans.

The French eat a lot of cheese and pastries and also suffer fewer heart attacks than the British or Americans.

The Italians eat starchy pasta and drink excessive amounts of red wine and also suffer fewer heart attacks than the British or Americans.

The Germans drink a lot of beer and eat lots of sausages and fats and suffer fewer heart attacks than the British or Americans.

The truth about eating fat and heart attacks is you can eat and drink what you like: speaking English is apparently what kills you.

The good and bad fats.

All fats are not the same; some are good and should be included in our diet. Eating the right kind of fat is important because dietary fat gets much of the blame for causing heart disease – the number one killer in the United States. Here's how to spot the good fats. Look for the prefix "UN," as in poly**un**saturated and mono**un**saturated fats.

The good fat, the unsaturated fat, is the basic energy fuel and a building block for body cells and tissues. Polyunsaturated fats are good fats found in wild game meat, and especially fatty fish like mackerel, salmon and sardines. It is also in oils made from safflower, sunflower, corn, soybean and wheat germ.

The bad fats are the saturated fats, also referred to as polysaturated fats, and the trans fats. They are abundant in meat and animal fat, dairy products, and a few vegetable oils like palm and coconut oil. Most packaged snack foods, like cookies, cakes, donuts and crackers, are high in trans fats. Food manufacturers are now required to list trans fats on food labels.

Red meat is NOT bad for you. Now blue-green meat, THAT'S bad for you!

Tommy Smothers

*"Excuse me, but which is it that practically kills you—
polysaturated or polyunsaturated?"*

Trans fats were discovered a century ago when food chemists found they could solidify unsaturated vegetable oil by heating it in the presence of hydrogen and finely ground particles of nickel metal. The process is called partial hydrogenation.

"Without this process," Harvard's Dr. Willett says, "we wouldn't have had margarine or vegetable shortenings like Crisco. We would also have less heart disease."

Eat properly.

A man walks into the psychiatrist's office with a cucumber up his nose, a carrot in his left ear and a banana in his right ear and he says, "What's the matter with me?" The psychiatrist says, "You're not eating properly."

Portion control. Portions in restaurants are often oversized, and a single meal can contain your daily allowance of calories. Consider sharing entrées or just enjoying an appetizer and a salad.

Minimize temptation. Don't stock your fridge and cabinet with carbonated sodas or high-calorie foods that will spike your blood sugar levels. Instead, keep a supply of almonds, walnuts, dried or fresh fruit for snacking.

Make lunch your main meal. People who are retired should consider eating their big meal at midday. Jennifer Workman, a registered dietitian and author of *Stop Your Cravings*, says, "Ayurveda is India's 5,000-year-old approach to wellness. According to ayurveda, we're designed to eat the larger meal at lunch because our digestive 'fire,' called *agni*, is strongest between 10 a.m. and 2 p.m., so we digest more efficiently. In my practice, I've seen people lose 5 to 10 pounds just by doing this."

Don't dig your grave with your own knife and fork.
English proverb

Beware of desserts. A single portion of the Cheesecake Factory's original cheesecake contains 800 calories and 28 grams of saturated fat. Try fruit for dessert, or order extra forks and share.

> *Do not worry; eat three square meals a day; say your prayers; be courteous to your creditors; keep your digestion good; exercise; go slow and easy. Maybe there are other things your special case requires to make you happy, but my friend, these I reckon will give you a good lift.*
> Abraham Lincoln

Stressed spelled backwards is desserts. Coincidence? I think not!

Anonymous

The world's wackiest diets.

The Large Dosage Diet: The FDA has approved pills that help you lose weight by making you feel full. The recommended dosage is five thousand pills a day.

The Valium Diet: With the Valium diet, you take three for breakfast and the rest of the day the food keeps falling out of your mouth.

The Easy-To-Stick-To Diet: You eat whatever you want whenever you want, and as much as you want. You won't lose any weight, but it's really easy to stick to.

The Drinker's Diet: You lose weight and your driver's license.

The McDonald's Diet: George Carlin says, "'Breakfast for Under a Dollar' actually costs much more than that. You have to factor in the cost of coronary bypass surgery."

The Grapefruit Diet: "I was on the grapefruit diet," said Max Alexander. "For breakfast I ate fifteen grapefruit. Now when I go to the bathroom I keep squirting myself in the eye."

The Genesis Diet: And God populated the earth with broccoli and cauliflower and spinach, green and yellow vegetables of all kinds, so Man and Woman would live long and healthy lives.

And Satan created McDonald's. And McDonald's brought forth the 99-cent double-cheeseburger. And Satan said to Man, "You want fries with that?" And Man said, "Super-size them." And Man gained pounds.

And God created the healthful yogurt, that Woman might keep her figure that man found so fair.

And Satan froze the yogurt, and he brought forth chocolate, nuts and brightly colored candies to put on the yogurt. And Woman gained pounds.

And God said, "Try my crispy fresh salad."

And Satan brought forth creamy dressings, bacon bits, and shredded cheese. And there was ice cream for dessert. And Woman gained more pounds.

And God said, "I have sent you heart-healthy vegetables and olive oil with which to cook them."

Diets are for those who are thick and tired of it.
Anonymous

And Satan brought forth chicken-fried steak so big it needed its own platter. And Man gained pounds, and his bad cholesterol went through the roof.

And God brought forth running shoes, and Man resolved to lose those extra pounds.

And Satan brought forth cable TV with remote control so Man would not have to toil to change channels between ESPN and EPSN2. And Man gained pounds.

And God brought forth the potato, a vegetable naturally low in fat and brimming with nutrition.

And Satan peeled off the healthful skin and sliced the starchy center into chips and deep fried them. And he created sour cream dip also. And Man clutched his remote control and ate the potato chips swaddled in cholesterol.

And Satan saw and said, "It is good." And Man went into cardiac arrest.

And God sighed and created quadruple bypass surgery.

And Satan created HMOs.

The Genesis Diet, author unknown

5

Choose a job you love and never have to work again.

*It is well with me only when
I have a chisel in my hand.*
Michelangelo

*Do what you love,
love what you do,
leave the world a better place
and don't pick your nose.*
Jeff Mallett

*"I'm a gladiator, but that's just to put food on the table.
What I really want to do is teach."*

For an increasing number of Americans, retirement means you may have to forget the golf clubs and the cruises and continue to work.

Johnny Carson advised, "Never continue in a job you don't enjoy. If you're happy in what you're doing you'll like yourself, you'll have inner peace. And if you have that, along with physical health, you will have had more success than you could possibly have imagined."

If you fail to plan, you plan to fail

You plan everything in life, and then the roof caves in on you because you haven't done enough thinking about who you are and what you should do with the rest of your life.

Lee Iacocca

Don't leave the future to chance and assume that after you stop working, all will fall comfortably into place.

In Alice in Wonderland, Alice said, "If you don't know where you're going, any road will take you there."

Is your plan to work for pay, full-time? Yes____No____
Is your plan to work for pay, part-time? Yes____No____
Is your plan to be in business for yourself? Yes___ No____
Is your plan to volunteer your services? Yes____No____

*A goal without a
plan is just a wish.*

Larry Elder

How can you get very far,
If you don't know who you are?
How can you do what you ought,
If you don't know what you've got?
And if you don't know which to do
Of all the things in front of you,
Then what you'll have when you
are through
Is just a mess without a clue
Of all the best that can come true
If you know what and which and who.

Cottleston Pie, from *The Tao of Pooh*
by Benjamin Hoff

Recognize your emotional needs.
If retirement means no longer doing things you love, it will
not be a happy experience. People underestimate the things
they like about their work. Many retirees miss the positive
reinforcement of structure, recognition, friendships, mental
stimulation, creativity, responsibility, being part of the
action, and job satisfaction.

The Old Man and the Oranges

Maurice was a mild-mannered man in the paper box
business. He was a planner, a thrifty, financially astute
businessman. His company rose to prominence in the
packaging industry. Maurice announced that he planned to
retire and spend part of the year in Florida.

Maurice purchased a modest, one-bedroom
apartment on Collins Avenue overlooking the Intercoastal

Waterway. In the evenings he would sit on the balcony enjoying his cigars. Once a week Maurice went to the race track and to Junior's Restaurant on Collins Avenue for a high cholesterol, hot pastrami sandwich. Life was good.

Three months later, Maurice contacted the company in which he still had stock and was the Honorary Chairman of the Board. "Your inventory is too high," he complained. "Your accounts receivable are out of kilter," he griped. "I'd better come home and check things out." And he did.

The company management was pleased to find Maurice surprisingly conciliatory when he returned for his one-week-per-month visit.

He confided to a company executive, "You know, at the office, they call me Mr. Maurice. I have the sailfish that I caught in Mexico hanging on the wall behind my desk. I'm respected, I'm somebody. In Florida, I'm just another old man waiting in line at the supermarket for oranges."

Retirement could not provide the pleasurable feelings of accomplishment and self-worth that he received from his work contributions.

Mr. Maurice continued to work at his desk until he died at 84. He believed that for him to be valued, respected, and appreciated was somehow interconnected with his job status. He was so wrong. I still miss my father.

What kind of a job do you want?

For baby boomers and all seniors who plan to continue working, now is an opportunity to identify your personal talents, interests, and experience and apply them to the kind of work that you are interested in engaging in.

What is it that you like doing? If you don't like it, get out of it, because you'll be lousy at it.

Lee Iacocca

"Have you given much thought to what kind of job you want after you retire?"

If you find a job that utilizes your interests, talents and experience, chances are you'll become completely absorbed. This pleasurable state of mind, or flow, is a feeling of such engagement and focus that time seems to pass unnoticed.

Employing your personal strengths enables you to make full, part-time, or volunteer job choices that will release positive energy, provide job satisfaction and even make you glad to get up in the morning.

Identify your special talents, experience and interests.
A talent is an attribute you were born with; for example, a natural singing voice, a photographic memory, a strong physique or a high IQ. Experience is the wisdom and skill gained over the years in the performance of your vocation or avocation.

1 What are your unique talents?

_____

_____

_____

_____

2 What is your special experience?

_____

_____

_____

When a man is happy, he does not hear the clock strike.

German proverb

3 What things do you most enjoy doing?

_____

_____

_____

_____

4 What things would you like to do that you're not doing now?

_____

_____

_____

_____

Far and away the best prize that life has to offer is the chance to work hard at work worth doing.

Theodore Roosevelt

5 If you could design the perfect dream job in terms of skills, responsibilities, work settings, and the people you work with, what would that job be?

_____

_____

_____

_____

My dream job assessment:

I inventoried my talents, experience and interests. For 40 years, I was in the packaging business. In 1993 the company I headed went bankrupt. So, being a business advisor is not high up on my list.

I reviewed my life experiences. In the Army, I was expert with a rifle. In Korea, I spent a month as an instructor in the 25th Division sniper school. This experience doesn't seem practical today, since I do not wish to lead African safaris or rob 7-Eleven stores, and besides, I have cataracts and don't see so good.

One of the things I most enjoyed in school was doodling cartoons, instead of paying close attention. My parents took remedial and preemptive action and sent me to Staunton Military Academy, where they beat me with wooden paddles for doodling.

Somehow, I survived and became editor of the Staunton yearbook, the *Shrapnel*, which I filled with cartoons. What then could be a better dream job in retirement than to write a book with cartoons, and even better, to be able to select from the best of the 68,643 cartoons ever published in *The New Yorker*. Releasing all this positive energy would provide job satisfaction.

I rushed to share the good news with my wife, Fran. "Dear," I said. "I have discovered that my talent and interest coincide and by using them every day in writing a book about retirement, I will receive abundant gratification and success. Isn't that great?"

I never did a day's work in my life. It was all fun.

Thomas A. Edison

I was a bank teller.
That was a great job.
I was bringing home
$450,000 a week.

Joe Lindley

"That's nice," Fran said. "Could you use some of your special talents and put the dirty laundry in the washing machine?"

I called my closest friend, who is a little hard-of-hearing. "Bob," I said. "I've made a discovery. We all have interests and talents that if we identify and..."

"What?" Bob said. "Speak up!"

"WE ALL HAVE TALENTS AND INTERESTS THAT..."

"I'm on my way to play tennis," Bob said. "I'll call you later."

I wanted to share this exciting news with my family. I phoned my eldest son, Jamie, who lives in Dallas.

"Your call is very important to me..." the answering machine began—I hung up.

I called my middle son, Scott, in New York.

"Hi. This is Scott. I'm either on the phone or away from my desk." I hung up again.

I knew that Adam, our youngest, would be at his store, *AMano*, in Washington. I called and one of his sales ladies answered. "Can I speak to Adam please?" I said.

"Adam is with a customer. Can I take a message?"

Frustrated, I said, "YES. Tell him his father is on the phone. I've just been diagnosed with a fatal disease and have only two minutes to live. I called to say goodbye."

There was a pause. "I'm sorry," she said. "What did you say your name was?"

"You seem reasonably fit—have you ever pulled a rickshaw?"

Find the right job.

> *The major difference between successful and unsuccessful job-hunters is not some factor out there such as a tight job market, but the way they go about their job hunt.*
>
> Richard N. Bolles, *What Color is Your Parachute?*

The Library of Congress chose *What Color is Your Parachute?* as one of the 25 books that have shaped readers' lives, and the *New York Times* said, "*Parachute* remains the most complete career guide around." It is a must-read.

Author Richard N. Bolles offers some valuable tips for a successful full, part-time, or volunteer job hunt.

The only place where success comes before work is a dictionary.
Vidal Sassoon

*   No one owes you a job. If you want a job, you are going to have to go out and hunt for it—hard. Your success will be in direct proportion to your job hunting effort.

*   The one thing a job-hunter needs above everything else is hope, and hope is born of persistence. Forget "what's available out there." Go after the job you really want.

*   Once you know what kind of work you are looking for, tell everyone what it is; have as many eyes and ears out there looking on your behalf as possible.

*You'll always miss 100%
of the shots you don't take.*

Wayne Gretzky

* At any organization, identify who has the power to hire you for the position you want, and use your friends' and acquaintances' contacts to get you in to see the person.

* Don't be wearied by rejection. Tom Jackson's model of the typical job hunt in his book *Guerrilla Tactics* is:
NO NO NO NO NO NO NO NO NO NO NO
NO NO NO NO NO NO NO NO NO NO NO
NO NO NO NO NO NO NO NO NO NO NO
NO NO NO NO NO NO NO NO NO NO NO
NO NO NO **YES!**

6

Stay connected to your family and friends.

*Call it a clan, call it a network, call it a tribe,
call it a family: Whatever you call it, whoever
you are, you need one.*
Jane Howard

*There can be no happiness
equal to the joy of finding
a heart that understands.*
Victor Robinson

*I never promised you
a smile
or taste of me
with your morning coffee
Wherever, Whenever.
I did however,
promise you
rainbows and lilacs
out of season
and Time, Time love,
to grow old with you.*

*I never promised
to graft my flesh
to yours
and live inside your head
Whenever, Wherever.
I did, however
promise you
a song,
and Time, Time love,
to grow old with you.*
Fran Mahr

How to divorce-proof your marriage.

Sex when you're married is like going to the 7-Eleven: There's not much variety but at three in the morning it's always there.

Carol Leifer

In a successful marriage, there is no such thing as one's way. There is only the way of both, only the bumpy, dusty, difficult but always mutual path.

Phyllis McGinley, Pulitzer Prize Winner

In 2004, my book *What Makes a Marriage Work* was published by Durban House Publishing Company. In an attempt to boost sales, the publisher arranged for Fran and me to be interviewed on radio stations—after all, we've been married for over 55 years.

I explained to the publisher that there are times my wife and I want to kill each other and that I don't understand women.

"Who does?" the publisher said. "All you gotta say on the interview is, 'Divorce is epidemic and we're sharing what we've learned after a half-century of marriage.' The interviews are conducted from your home. The phone rings at the appointed time and you're on the air.

"Give 'em a list of things," she said, "make some funny. That's all there is to it."

The Playboy satellite channel. Our very first radio interview was with Tiffany Granath, the famous Playboy Playmate and celebrity host of Playboy's Sirius Satellite radio program.

I researched Tiffany's web site for adults only and was terrified of the embarrassing questions she might ask. I prepared pages of answers and had a stiff scotch before the studio called.

"Fran," I said, "we should rehearse a little."

"Why?" she said. "I'm a professional, I've done hundreds of radio spots. Just relax and have fun. Don't be so uptight."

At the appointed time, the phone rang. The producer said, "I'll patch you into the live broadcast and Tiffany will introduce you in a few minutes."

As we listened to the show in progress, a phone-in caller was graphically describing an anal sex problem, asking Tiffany for advice. Fran's eyes grew wide as saucers. My palms got sweaty.

"And now I would like to introduce our guests, Frances and Malcolm Mahr," Tiffany said. "I read Malcolm's book *What Makes a Marriage Work*, and it is a wonderful book about marriage. Now let's open the phones for your questions. Here's Stan calling from California."

"Tiffany," the caller said. "My problem is that my wife always told me that if I ever had sex with anyone else, I should tell her. Well, Tiffany, I just had incredible sex, now I'm driving home and talking on my cell phone. Should I tell my wife?"

"Well...Stan," Tiffany said, "since – "

"Excuse me, Tiffany," Fran said. "There's different strokes for different folks. Maybe your wife is getting her kicks – "

My systolic blood pressure rose to advanced hypertension.

"Excuse me, Fran," said Tiffany. "Stan, if your wife asked you to tell her, then perhaps you shouldn't keep it buried."

At one point in the show, I asked if Tiffany would like to hear my sexual fantasy. She had no choice but to say, "Okay."

"It's my birthday," I said, "and Fran comes into the

Do you know what it means to come home at night to a woman who'll give you a little love, a little affection, a little tenderness? It means you're in the wrong house, that's what it means.

Henny Youngman

bedroom wearing a skimpy, sexy outfit and says, 'Honey, for your birthday, you can do anything you want to me.'

"I would say, 'Really, anything?' Then I would tie her hands and feet to the bedposts and go out and play golf."

"That's funny," Tiffany said to be polite. And then the "Tiffany and Fran Show" continued giving advice to callers.

...more radio interviews. Following Fran's being discovered on the national Playboy satellite channel, we were invited to be interviewed by a radio station in Idaho with an audience of 9,316. I was introduced following a long car wash commercial.

"And our next guest," said Mike, the host, "is Malcolm Mahr, author of *What Makes a Marriage Work*. Hi, Malcolm, welcome to the show."

Mac: "Thank you, Mike, and with me is my wife, Fran."

Mike: "Oh? Did she help you write the book, Malcolm?"

Mac: "That's right, Mike. Without Fran's help, the book would have been finished a year earlier."

Mike: "Heh, heh. Well hello, Fran."

Fran: "Hello, Mike. I was only eighteen when I was married. I was planning to go to New York to be on the stage – "

Mike: "Excuse me, Fran. Malcolm, what do you think is most important about marriage?"

Mac: "Our friendship has been the glue that has – "

Fran: "Would you like to hear me sing, Mike?"

Mike: "Heh, heh. Malcolm, what else is important?"

Mac: "Laughter is also important. We have to be able to laugh more, particularly at ourselves. There is a wonderful

My mom always said, "Men are like linoleum floors. You lay them right, and you can walk on them for thirty years."

Brett Butler

quote by Paul Newman's wife, Joanne Woodward, that Fran will read..."

(Sound of shuffling of papers)

Fran: "I can't find it."

Mike: "Let's get back to friendship."

Mac: "I think friendship is the best predictor of a good marriage. We like to go to movies, theater, and art shows together. Fran, tell them about the art show in the nudist colony."

Fran: "Which one?"

Mac: "THE ONE IN THE BOOK!"

Fran: "Right. Well, a friend of mine, Marie, is an artist. She does great work. She invited us to an art show. Mac, you tell him."

Mac: "As we walked to the car, we passed a tall, well-endowed gentleman walking down the lane – stark naked – talking on his cell phone. I said to Fran, 'Did you see that naked guy on the cell phone?' 'Cell phone?' she said. 'What cell phone?'"

Mike: (Silence) "This is a family channel," he said. "We don't want to lose our license. It was a pleasure having you on the show." CLICK!

Let there be spaces in your togetherness.
Most of us desire a certain amount of personal space. We need time to pursue individual interests. A healthy relationship is when partners not only have fulfilling lives and identities outside the relationship, but also encourage each other to do so.

For two people in marriage to live together day after day is unquestionably the one miracle the Vatican has overlooked.

Bill Cosby

"Jack and I have learned to accept each other's idiosyncrasies, like my passion for cashew brittle, and his going out every night and not coming home until dawn."

SIPRESS

"You haven't said anything for ten years. Is everything O.K.?"

Communicate your feelings.

Thinking is a rational exercise using our brains. Feelings are events utilizing our emotions. Personal feelings are neither right nor wrong. Is it wrong to feel cold, to feel hot, or to feel unhappy?

When a partner feels sad, depressed, hurt or worried, he or she is not responsive to logic or reason. Learning how to talk out personal feelings and be nonjudgmental in listening to each other are valuable attributes for a long-lasting relationship.

Marriage is really tough because you have to deal with feelings...and lawyers.
Richard Pryor

"You want a child, I want a dog. Can't we compromise?"

Making compromises is not losing.

Like it or not, the only solution to marital problems is to compromise. In a loving relationship it just doesn't work for either of you to get things all your way, even if you are convinced you're right. This would create such iniquity and unfairness that the marriage would suffer.
John Gottman, *Why Marriages Succeed or Fail*

Without being listened to, we are shut up in the solitude of our own hearts.
Michael P. Nichols

Listen, Listen, Listen.
Listening has two purposes: the taking in of information and providing your mate the validation essential for sustaining self-respect. He or she wants to feel understood, and not ignored, unappreciated, or cut off and alone.

The Golden Rule of marriage: *Be kind to one another.*
When people ask, "You've been married over fifty years and you wrote the book about marriage; what's your advice?" I respond that I honestly don't know the answers to a successful marriage.

You have to be lucky enough to find the right partner, and sometimes you have to take a deep breath, "pull-up-your-socks, suck-it-in," and be there when you're needed.

If there are Golden Rules of marriage, at the the top of my list, other than luck, would be the importance of being friends, sharing feelings, and most of all, being kind to one another.

To love a person is to learn the song in their heart and to sing it to them when they have forgotten.
Thomas Chandler

Enrich your marital relationship: *Marriage Encounter*
We spend a lot of time and money on maintaining our homes, our vehicles, our clothing, our careers...but how much time do we spend maintaining our marriage? Marriage Encounter invites married couples of all faiths to rediscover their marriage through a unique method of dialogue, personal reflection, and mutual sharing of feelings. Fran and I attended Marriage Encounter. IT WORKS! Call **800-828-3351.**

"I'm in the sandwich generation—my parents don't approve of me and my kids hate me."

The reason grandparents and grandchildren get along so well is that they have a common enemy.

Sam Levenson

The Sandwich Generation.
This is the generation of middle-aged men and women who are tightly sandwiched between the needs and problems of their children migrating toward independence and the needs and problems of their aging parents drifting toward dependency.

Letting go.

For children, letting go from parents is a necessary, but often difficult, step toward maturity. Freud described detachment from parental authority as the most significant and most painful psychic achievement of adolescence.

For parents, letting go means giving up control – or the illusion that we ever had it. In his classic, *The Prophet*, Kahlil Gibran counseled, "You are the bows from which your children are sent forth. Let your bending be for gladness, for even as he loves the arrow that flies, so he loves the bow that is stable."

The best way to keep children home is to make the home atmosphere pleasant – and let the air out of the tires.

Dorothy Parker

When our youngest son, Adam, was thirteen years old, his school's art class was taking an overnight trip. The morning of the excursion, Adam kissed his mother goodbye and I accompanied him to meet the minivan driven by his art teacher. When the beautiful, young brunette art teacher stepped out to greet me, I was startled to view her statuesque figure, and my eyes riveted to her large, melon-shaped breasts.

Returning to the house, I said to Fran, "Wow. You should have seen Adam's art teacher."

"Why do you say that?" said Fran.

"She looked like this," I said, stretching my hands in front of my chest, palms up and opened wide, fingertips curled.

"You mean the poor woman had arthritis?"

"Not exactly, dear," I replied.

If Kahlil Gibran's young son had gone off on a trip with an art teacher that had a knockout figure like my son Adam's did, I'm not so sure how much gladness would have been in *his* letting go.

The Empty Nest Syndrome.

When the day comes that our children leave, we are filled with mixed emotions: finally we will have the place all to ourselves and we won't sleep fitfully until we hear their footsteps arriving home at 3 A.M. – from God knows where.

On the other hand, we worry whether they will find the right person to love; we worry whether they will have a decent roof over their heads; we worry whether they will be able to fulfill their personal goals; and we worry about how to get them home again to visit.

Happiness is having a large, loving, caring, close-knit family in another city.

George Burns

An elderly man in Miami calls his son in New York and says, "I hate to ruin your day, but I have to tell you that your mother and I are divorcing. Forty-five years of misery is enough!"

"Pop, what are you talking about?" the son screams.

"We can't stand the sight of each other any longer!" the old man says. "We're sick of each other, and I'm sick of talking about this, so you call your sister in Chicago and tell her." He hangs up.

Frantic, the son calls his sister, who explodes on the phone. "They are not getting divorced," she shouts. "I'll take care of this!" She immediately calls her father and screams at the old man, "You are NOT getting divorced! Don't do a single thing until I get there! I'm calling my brother back. We'll both be there tomorrow. Until then, don't do a thing. DO YOU HEAR ME?" She hangs up.

The old man hangs up the phone, smiles and turns to his wife. "Okay," he says, "they're coming for the holidays and paying their own airfares."

The Boomerang Phenomenon: "They're back."

Did your kids speed out the door on their way to college and freedom, only to ricochet back after not finding a job right away? It's called the Boomerang Phenomenon.

Based upon the 2000 U.S. Census data, about 25 percent of Americans between the ages of 18 and 34 now live with their parents. This, the twenty-something generation, is characterized as marrying later, divorcing faster, staying in school longer, competing for jobs in a retrenching economy, and being priced out of the expensive real estate market.

Human beings are the only creatures on earth that allow their children to come back home.

Bill Cosby

"Your mother and I think it's time you got a place of your own. We'd like a little time alone before we die."

Appreciation can make a day-even change a life. Your willingness to put it into words is all that's necessary.

Margaret Cousins

We all need attention.

In *The Sandwich Generation*, Michael Zal discusses parent-adolescent relationships. "During early childhood," Zal says, "the key to parenting was to give love. During latency, it was to set limits. During adolescence, a helpful parent must learn to listen." He includes a poem, "Listen," by an anonymous writer.

Listen

When I ask you to listen to me and you start
giving advice,
you have not done what I asked.
When I ask you to listen and you begin
to tell me why
I shouldn't feel that way, you are trampling
on my feelings.
When I ask you to listen to me and you feel you
have to do
something to solve my problems, you have failed
me, strange
as that may seem.
Perhaps that's why prayer works for some people
Because
God is mute and He doesn't offer advice or try
to fix things.
He just listens and trusts you to work it out
for yourself.
So please, just listen and hear me. And if you want
to talk, wait a few minutes for your turn and I
promise I'll listen to you.

Anonymous

With the gift of listening comes the gift of healing.

Catherine de Hueck

To put the world in order, we must first put the nation in order; to put the nation in order, we must first put the family in order; to put the family in order, we must first cultivate our personal life; we must first set our hearts right.

Confucius

We all need love.
We all need love, and if children don't find it at home they will seek it elsewhere.

Families are like fudge... mostly sweet with a few nuts.

Anonymous

A teenager brought home her new boyfriend to meet her parents, and they were appalled by his appearance: leather jacket, motorcycle boots, tattoos and a pierced nose. Later, the parents pulled their daughter aside and said, "He doesn't seem very nice."

"Mom," replied the daughter, "if he wasn't so nice, why would he be doing 5000 hours of community service?"

"My son is a saint—he's always coöperating with the authorities."

We all need recognition.
It's good to get in the habit of looking for what's good in our children. Building them up is more effective then tearing them down. Nothing feels better than receiving *empathic* listening, genuine praise and *sincere* expressions of love from parents.

> *There are only four kinds of people in the world:*
> *Those who have been caregivers*
> *Those who currently are caregivers*
> *Those who will be caregivers*
> *Those who will need caregivers*
> Former First Lady
> Rosalynn Carter

Caring for aging parents.
The elderly are rapidly becoming the largest segment of our population. In the next twenty years the number of people over sixty-five will rise from thirty-five to fifty million, and the number over eighty-five will be sixteen million. For each of these elderly persons there will likely be a family member caught in the Sandwich Generation. It is a daunting challenge. In time, the

emotional and physical dependence of aging parents will increase. Roles will reverse as you become your parents' caregiver.

Three sons left home, went out on their own and prospered. Getting back together, they discussed the gifts they were able to give their elderly mother.

The first said, "I built a big house for our mother."

The second said, "I sent a new Mercedes and a driver."

The third smiled and said, "I've got you both beat. You know how Mom enjoys the Bible, and you know she can't see very well. I sent her a parrot that can recite the entire Bible. It took 20 monks in a monastery 12 years to teach him. I had to pledge to contribute $100,000 a year for 10 years, but it was worth it. Mom just has to name the chapter and verse and the parrot will recite it."

Soon thereafter, Mom sent out her letters of thanks:

"Milton," she wrote the first son, "the house you built is so huge. I live in only one room, but I have to clean the whole house."

"Marvin," she wrote the second son, "I'm too old to travel. I stay home all the time, so I never use the Mercedes. And the driver is rude!"

"My dearest Melvin," she wrote to her third son, "you were the only son to have the good sense to know what your mother likes. The chicken was delicious."

...Mom

The family seems to have two predominant functions: to provide warmth and love in time of need and to drive each other insane.

Donald G. Smith

Alzheimer's.

Alzheimer's is a disease, not a natural result of aging. It is a deterioration of the brain, which results in chronic loss of memory and personality changes. The cause of Alzheimer's is unknown – there is no cure. It's a progressive illness that robs its victims of the ability to think, reason, and function in everyday life.

Nobody, as long as he moves about among the chaotic currents of life, is without trouble.

Carl Jung

Tick Tock

We walked through the doors
touching,
Only her cane separating us.
She smiled,
her calloused fingers grazed along my arm.
We sat and waited.
Time, she used to remember well
Tick Tock, Tick Tock.
The shabby bag resting between us
held clothes, a comb, slippers and her Bible
neatly stacked
nothing to hide
"Mother," I said, "it's time."

Fran Mahr

My 96-year-old mother-in-law, Bess, died this year. She suffered with raging Alzheimer's disease. Twelve years before, when Bess first moved into an assisted care facility, she was outspoken, opinionated and readily shared her feelings. I suggested we take our video camera and record an interview with "Mommie Bessie," as she was called by her family.

Ripping out the last page of Vanity Fair magazine, I copied down and modified some interview questions: "What are your early recollections of growing up in Annapolis?" "What was your favorite journey?" "What do you consider your greatest achievement?" "How did you meet your husband, Harry?"

Bess was dressed for the occasion in a pretty red dress; her hair looked beautiful. I did the videotaping, Fran did the interviewing. Bess was enjoying the attention and the idea of being on camera. Near the end of the taping Fran improvised with a question of her own. "How do you like living here?" Fran asked.

"I HATE IT HERE!" Bess sputtered. "AND YOU MADE ME COME HERE. IT'S ALL YOUR FAULT!"

I stopped videotaping.

Caregiving is heart work.

Caring for your parents may be the most difficult task you will ever face – physically, emotionally, and psychologically.

In his book *When Bad Things Happen to Good People*, Rabbi Harold S. Kushner says, "The helplessness of aging parents, their appeals to their children, tap feelings of inadequacy, buried resentment, and guilt in many perfectly decent people. It is a hard situation to handle under the best of circumstances."

Caregivers are already carrying a heavy burden. They do not need to feel further weighed down with guilt. Being resentful and having angry feelings doesn't mean you're a bad person or hate your parent. It means the situation is stressful.

In Alzheimer's (disease) the mind dies first: Names, dates, places – the interior scrapbook of an entire life fades into mists of non recognition.

Matt Clark

Don't neglect the quality of your own life or others in your household. Even if you're working, make time to rest, relax, and exercise. Plan some long weekends to recharge your batteries. Your emotional and physical health is important. If you see signs that either you or your spouse are getting seriously depressed, get professional help. The textbook definition of depression is anger turned inward instead of being discharged outward.

Caregiving can be hard work, emotionally draining and sometimes, terribly sad. But caring is what human beings and families do and have done for generations.

I've learned that every day you should reach out and touch someone. People love a warm hug, or just a freindly pat on the back.

Maya Angelou

The importance of family support.
In 1997, Mitch Albom wrote *Tuesdays with Morrie*, a chronicle of conversations with his old psychology professor at Brandeis College, Morrie Schwartz. Morrie had a fatal illness, ALS or Lou Gehrig's disease, a brutal, unforgiving failure of the neurological system. The author shares Morrie's lasting wisdom with the world. When I finished reading and stopped crying, I sent a copy to each of our three sons.

There is no secure ground upon which people may stand if it isn't family. Love is important. Without love, we are birds with broken wings. And family is not just love, but knowing there's someone watching out for you. Nothing else gives you that. Not money. Not work. Not fame.

Morrie Schwartz, *Tuesdays with Morrie*

If a man does not make new acquaintances as he advances through life, he will soon find himself left alone; one should keep his friendships in constant repair.

Dr. Samuel Johnson

"Hello, cutie pie."

Close relationships enhance your well-being.

The MacArthur Foundation worked with the best scientific minds in the country to research the aging process. The results validate the linking of social relationships to health, citing, "For people whose relationships with others are few, the risk of suicide or other causes of death is two to four times greater, irrespective of age, race, smoking, physical health, use of alcohol, physical activity, or socioeconomic status."

The Judge

Last year Fran and I attended the funeral of an old friend, a 76-year-old retired judge, Robert Hammerman.

Early one morning on Veterans' Day, Bob Hammerman walked to a wooded area near his home and shot himself with a gun he had purchased for that purpose.

"I owe you an explanation," began a letter he had mailed a day before to more than 2,200 people. Bob had decided to end his life more than a year earlier primarily because of his growing concern that he had Alzheimer's disease. More than death, the elderly bachelor said he feared losing his memory and his independence.

His suicide was reported in newspapers around the country. A cum laude graduate from Johns Hopkins, a graduate from Harvard University Law School, and the longest-serving judge in Maryland history, Bob was also well-known for his stewardship of the Lancers, a leadership and service organization, that spanned seven decades.

"How could he do this?" I asked his closest friend, Sam, at the funeral. "Did he really have Alzheimer's?"

Sam, a doctor, shrugged and said, "I don't know. Despite his relationship with over 2,000 people, Bob had few close friends. He thought he would end up living alone with no one to help take care of him in his old age."

True friendship is like sound health, the value of it is seldom known until it be lost.

Charles Caleb Colton

Whether a baby boomer or a retired judge, human beings are not meant to live solitary lives. Close relationships can promote both physical and psychological well-being.

A study of over a thousand heart patients at Duke University's medical center found people without a spouse or close confidant were three times more likely to die within five years of heart disease as those who were married or had a close friend. Duke University's medical researchers all reached the same conclusion: "Close relationships do, in fact, promote health."

Instead of just loving our enemies, we should treat our friends a little better.

Anonymous

In the beginning of life, when we are infants, we need others to survive, right? And at the end of life, when you get like me, you need others to survive, right? But here's the secret: in between we need others as well.

Morrie Schwartz, interviewed shortly before his death by Mitch Albom in *Tuesdays with Morrie*

Make new friends but keep the old.
We never outgrow our need for friends. The health benefits of close social ties hold throughout life. The MacArthur report confirms that, in general, married people live longer than unmarried people. Members of religious and secular organizations live longer than people without such group affiliations. Older women who report little opportunity to talk to others about their problems tend to have higher blood pressure than those with close friends. Men who reported high social support and good friends had lower levels of stress hormones.

Make new friends, but keep the old;
Those are silver, these are gold.
New-made friends, like new-made wine,
Age will mellow and refine.
Friendships that have stood the test—
of time and change – are surely best;
Brow may wrinkle, hair may gray,
Friendship never knows decay.
For 'mid old friends, tried and true,
Once more our youth renew.
But old friends, alas! may die,
New friends must their place supply.
Cherish friendship in your breast—
New is good, but old is best;
Make new friends, but keep the old;
Those are silver, these are gold.

Unknown

There are two things people want more than sex and money...recognition and praise.
Mary Kay Ash

Five surefire ways to make new friends—at any age.
1 Be a good listener and let others talk about themselves.

You can make more friends in two months by being interested in other people than you can in two years trying to get other people interested in you.

Dale Carnegie

2 Make the other person feel important – and do it sincerely.

Pretend that every person you meet has a sign around his or her neck that says, "Make Me Feel Important." Not only will you succeed in sales, you will succeed in life.

Mary Kay Ash, founder, Mary Kay Cosmetics

If you go looking for a friend, you're going to find they're very scarce. If you go out to be a friend, you'll find them everywhere.

Zig Ziglar

3 If you see someone without a smile, give them yours.

A smile costs nothing but gives much. It enriches those who receive without making poorer those who give. It takes but a moment, but the memory of it sometimes lasts forever. Yet a smile cannot be bought, begged, borrowed, or stolen, for it is something that is of no value to anyone until it is given away. Some people are too tired to give you a smile. Give them one of yours.

Anonymous

4 Remember that a person's name is to that person the sweetest and most important sound in any language.

As a Dale Carnegie graduate, I had learned a technique to remember people's names by association. At a party, I was seated with my wife and other guests. *Aha,* I thought, *I'll memory-associate everyone's name.*

Introducing myself and Fran, I tried to remember each person's name connected to a vivid memory-association. A willowy young charmer was seated across from me in a low-cut gown. Her name was Elizabeth.

I formed a mental image of her as Queen Elizabeth, topless, wearing a diamond tiara, scepter, and ermine. Ten minutes later, I looked across the table at the young lady, memory-associating her. *"Victoria,"* I said, "please pass the gravy."

If you want to win friends, make it a point to remember names. When you remember people's names, you pay them a subtle compliment; you indicate that they have made an impression on you. By using their names you add to their feelings of importance. But if you meet someone named Elizabeth, you're on your own.

5 *Do unto others as they'd like done unto them.* In his book *The Platinum Rule,* Tony Alessandra says, "A lot of good has been done in the world by people practicing the Golden Rule. As a guide for personal values, it can be a powerful force for honesty and compassion. But as a yardstick for communication, the Golden Rule has a downside."

Alessandra suggests that we honor the real intent of the Golden Rule by modifying that ancient maxim just a bit. "We think the secret to better relationships," says Alessandra, "is to apply the Platinum Rule: Do unto others as they'd like done unto them."

The Platinum Rule means learning to understand other people – and interacting with them in a way that's best for them, not just us. It means using our knowledge and our tact to put others at ease. "That," says Alessandra, "is the true spirit of the Golden Rule. So the Platinum Rule isn't at odds with the Golden Rule. Instead you might say it's a newer, more sensitive version."

The best vitamin for making friends is: B1.
Anonymous

Good neighbors provide emotional nourishment.
We never outgrow our need for good friends and good neighbors. Human beings are social creatures. We flourish in the company of other human beings.

Far better a neighbor that is near than a brother far off.
Proverbs 27:10

"I guess the Garcías won't be coming to visit anymore."

Don't wait to tell your friends how important they are.
Make a list of the people in your life in whose company you
feel more alive, happy, and comfortable. Contact them and
tell them how important they are to you. Don't assume they
already know it – even if they do – they would probably
love to learn it anyway. And don't wait until it is too late.

*Silent gratitude isn't very
much use to anyone.*
Gertrude Stein

*If with pleasure you are viewing
any work a friend is doing,
If you like him or you love him, tell him now;
Don't withhold your approbation
till the parson makes oration
And he lies with snowy lilies on his brow;
If you feel some praise is due him
now's the time to slip it to him,
For he cannot read his tombstone when he's dead.*

*More than fame and more than money
is the praise kind and sunny
And the hearty, warm approval of a friend.
If he earns your praise – bestow it;
if you like him let him know it;
Let the words of true encouragement be said.
Do not wait till life is over
and he's underneath the clover,
For he cannot read his tombstone when he's dead.*

Berton Braley

7

Be mindful of your finances – money matters.

I have enough money to last me the rest of my life, unless I buy something.

Jackie Mason

Money can't buy happiness, but neither can poverty.

Leo Rosten

"If we take a late retirement and an early death, we'll just squeak by."

The economy depends about as much on economists as the weather does on weather forecasters.

Jean-Paul Kauffmann

My 96-year-old mother-in-law, Bess, spent her last years in a nursing home suffering with Alzheimer's and other serious ailments. Ten years before her death in 2007, the family, with professional advice, had forecast and planned for her financial needs through a projected age of 93. Bess outlived the plan, and the ongoing costs of medicines and care depleted her assets.

It is a sobering experience to understand that a similar fate awaits many of us. It is obligatory to plan for your future financial security. In today's real world of increased health costs and potential cuts in Social Security, seniors know that money matters.

Protect your assets.
Protecting your assets is serious business. Especially for retirees, money represents security. To get the best advice on protecting your money, I interviewed one of America's best known retail stockbrokers, Julius Westheimer.

For more than 35 years as an investment broker, commentator, columnist, lecturer, and author of the book *Generation of Wealth*, Julius Westheimer gave straight advice without the jargon and posturing of his counterparts. He delivered time-tested rules for worry-free investing.

MAHR: With 76 million Americans and 10 million Canadian boomers moving toward retirement in the next few years, what advice do you offer these new retirees?

WESTHEIMER: We have been in the middle of an investment frenzy fueled by baby-boomers. They are doing it for their own protection. They are afraid that when they

"It's very important that you try very, very hard to remember where you electronically transferred Mommy and Daddy's assets."

If you would be wealthy, think of saving as well as getting.

Benjamin Franklin

retire inflation will have eroded their accumulated wealth; the national debt is worrisome, and Social Security benefits may be reduced. Retirees have enough adjustment problems in life without worrying about some foolish move that will wipe out your savings. You want to sleep at night knowing your money is protected.

Perhaps the market will continue to grow skywards in the years ahead, but as my father said, "Son, trees don't grow to the sky." I'm inclined to think that markets go in cycles, and if the market is predictable for one thing – it's unpredictability.

Financial planning for the future.

MAHR: When should retirees begin to plan for their future?

WESTHEIMER: I'll be the first to admit: it's hard to make plans for the future when so much is unsure. Few of us know how long we will live. People are outliving their forebears because they don't smoke, or because they exercise and watch their diet more carefully. The financial risk is that with better medicine and better nutrition, your money will run out before you do. The way to protect against that possibility is to have high quality stocks that raise their dividends every year to protect you against inflation.

MAHR: How can people educate themselves about high quality stocks and investing wisely?

Never spend your money before you have it.

Thomas Jefferson

WESTHEIMER: There are some excellent books on personal investing that I think we're still going to want to read years from now. *The Intelligent Investor*, by Benjamin Graham, tops that category. I also cite *One Up on Wall Street*, by Peter Lynch, because it's accessible to the average reader. As to TV, I don't act on anything I hear on television without first having my research department study it. The media, like everybody else, can sometimes be unreliable and the stakes for the investors are high.

No matter how many investment advice books you read, including mine, I advise you to have a broker or investment professional helping you. There is no replacement for personal contact with a broker who understands your goals and objectives.

MAHR: Why do we need a full-service broker when we can make transactions ourselves on the Internet for less than $10 a trade? Plus, you hear horror stories about unscrupulous brokers. They induce you to buy and sell when you shouldn't merely to generate fees, or they try to sell you inferior in-house investments with high commissions and mediocre returns.

Put not your trust in money, but put your money in trust.
Oliver Wendell Holmes

WESTHEIMER: A good broker can offer invaluable counsel, especially if you lack the experience, time or interest to do your own research. With the discounters, you pretty much get what you pay for – no advice, no research, no hand-holding. And in the case of online brokers it's worse: clogged servers, missing checks and long waits on customer service lines.

Choosing the right broker or investment counseling firm is crucial if you're going to delegate discretion to that professional.

MAHR: How do you suggest a broker be chosen?

WESTHEIMER: Here's what I recommend. If you know people who are successful investors and you respect their judgment, ask them to suggest a broker's name. Your accountant or lawyer is another reliable source.

When you meet the prospective broker, ask him or her these questions: Do you require a minimum amount of money to take on a new client and, if so, what is it? What stocks do you like now and why? What investments do you like for conservative growth, aggressive growth, and income? How long have you been a broker? What's your background? Can you furnish me client references? How often can I expect you to contact me and how often will I receive statements from you?

I often say, "Nobody cares as much about your money as you do." And it's true. It's your responsibility to make sure that the shape of your portfolio is right, and even more important, that it is adjusted as your needs change. It's fine to put your confidence in a broker, and it's the broker's responsibility to keep an eye on your portfolio, but the final responsibility is your own.

Money is better than poverty, if only for financial reasons.
Woody Allen

MAHR: Well, if it's our responsibility, do you have any tips?

WESTHEIMER: For every type of person, at every time and place in life, there is a different way to save and invest. Your readers must act based on their own situations and own aspirations. In my book *Generation of Wealth*, I explain time-tested rules for worry-free investing. One of the main ingredients of investor success is patience. It takes time to develop the right portfolio, and in reality, most investments take at least six months to a year to materialize.

Also, there are no emergencies in our business. There is no reason to be rushed into anything. Never. Any broker who tries to push you into signing on the dotted line right away should be viewed with a healthy degree of suspicion.

Westheimer's 6 rules for savvy investors.
1 The 120 rule: Take the number 120, and subtract your age from it. The resulting figure is roughly the percent of your investments that should be in common stocks. Most

investment is not about greed or need: it is about saving and earning money for the future.

2 Don't have too many stocks and don't have too few. Each stock you own should be no more than 5-10% of your portfolio. For appropriate diversion, you should hold about 20 stocks.

3 Stick to fundamentals. Emotions make the stock market unpredictable, but a solid company will generally prevail.

The mint makes it first, it is up to you to make it last.
Evan Esar

4 Use the company's dividends to figure out whether it is worth buying its stock. A company's regular and rising dividends can reassure you that, even if the stock is down, the company is doing well.

5 Pay attention to the Price / Earnings ratio. Use this concept to figure out the comparative cost and value of a stock. A high P/E ratio makes the stock more expensive, but sometimes it is worth paying for high growth. A too-high price earnings ratio might mean that the stock is overvalued – and therefore not a good buy.

6 Research departments can be useful, but their recommendations should be viewed cautiously. Remember, a high tide raises all ships, so when a stock goes up with a rising market, it isn't necessarily a winner. You should evaluate all information you read with a broker you trust.

Investment clubs.
MAHR: What do you think of investment clubs?

WESTHEIMER: Investment clubs are good for a number of financial, educational, and social reasons. You get together, you get your feet wet as an investor, you swap ideas, you meet new people, and you meet a new stock broker. There is also no rule that says you shouldn't make the same investment for your own personal accounts. If you are a small investor with too little time and confidence to invest alone, and not enough money for a mutual fund, consider an investment club.

Mutual funds.
MAHR: Do you like mutual funds?

The stock market is predictable for its unpredictability.

Julius Westheimer

WESTHEIMER: A mutual fund is nothing more than a collection of stocks that a money manager puts together, packages, and offers for sale. When it comes to relatively small amounts of money, $5,000 or less, I often recommend mutual funds because they provide two things the so-called average investor is unlikely to get on his own: diversification and professional management.

Mutual funds have become more important than ever before because of the growth in 401(k) plans. Mutual funds also help you get international stocks into your portfolio. This is a necessary part of diversification. Index mutual funds like the S&P 500 will generally do exactly what the market does. If you're relatively risk-adverse, they might be a good thing, but you can do better than that if you do your homework and work with your broker.

MAHR: I thought bonds were supposed to be secure, but

look at the knowledgeable people who lost money in Enron bonds.

WESTHEIMER: Enron is an unfortunate example of the importance of having diversification – not having everything tied up in one or two companies – and credit risk. Criminal fraud is difficult to guard against. Enron's filings with the IRS, SEC and other regulatory agencies were grossly exaggerated. This is the biggest, most complex case pending in district court in America right now, and shouldn't scare people away from bonds.

You should always live within your income, even if you have to borrow to do so.
Josh Billings

When you buy a bond, you are lending money to an organization, government or corporation who promises to pay you back the amount you invested, plus a specific rate of interest that never changes during the length of the bond. Some investors don't like the secure aspect of bonds. They think they are too young for bonds and want to make big hits. Some people would rather eat well than sleep well.

On the other hand, there are some folks who put almost all their money in bonds. Many of these investors suffered through the Depression, or lost everything in the stock market crash.

Certificates of Deposit.
MAHR: When do you recommend Certificates of Deposit?

WESTHEIMER: If someone comes to me with a definite foreseeable need – college, a house, a trip – I advise them to stay out of the stock market because the market could be 20% lower by the time the bills are due.

I may put that client's money in a five-year certificate

of deposit (CD), or a five-year government bond, to be sure the money will be there when the client needs it.

MAHR: With the baby boomers retiring to warmer climates, like Florida and Arizona, isn't real estate investing a good idea?

WESTHEIMER: If you're looking at alternate ways to invest your money, definitely take real estate and REIT's (Real Estate Investment Trusts) into consideration. If I were investigating a REIT myself, I would think mostly of the quality of the properties involved. The problem is, I don't know how to assess real estate. So, it's back to the basic rule of investing. Apply it as you would in selecting stocks: Is management any good?

MAHR: Westy, what's your favorite investment story?

WESTHEIMER: On TV, radio, and in newspapers, millions of Americans have read or listened to my advice over the years. This advice is what's worked for my clients. In some cases it's even worked for non-clients.

In 1987, I was sitting in my office when my phone rang. The man running the large pension fund for the State of Maryland employees was calling with a thank-you. "Westy," he said, "you saved Maryland $1 billion."

"How?" I asked.

"All of us were nervous about the market," he said, "and we wondered what to do. The state comptroller Louis Goldstein came into our pension board meeting and said, 'I just heard Julius Westheimer say on WBAL Radio that

My formula for success is rise early, work late and strike oil.

J.P. Getty

if you're terribly worried about your stocks, sell half of your positions.'

"That's what we did. One week before the October 1987 crash, we sold half of our portfolio and you saved us a fortune."

The Dow Five and Ten theories.

WESTHEIMER: Don't overlook the Dow Five and Ten theories. There are a few theories based on the Dow Jones Industrial Average that I'm actually beginning to think are foolproof. The theories are based on mathematical formulas and have been extremely profitable because of absolute adherence to their rules.

To get the Dow Five, first take the ten highest-yielding stocks on the Dow Jones Industrial Average; this is the Dow Ten.

Anyone can find them by reading the *Wall Street Journal.* Look for the ten Dow stocks with the highest dividend yield. Either find them yourself or ask a broker to find them for you.

From the ten highest-yielding stocks, extract the five lowest-priced ones, on the valid assumption that the lowest-priced stocks will recover quickly and thus rise more percentage-wise than higher-priced but lower-quality stocks. Then in equal dollar amounts, buy the five stocks with the lowest prices and highest yields.

Don't do anything for a whole year. Then, if nothing has changed, and these five Dow stocks are still the lowest

Mere wealth can't bring us happiness, mere wealth can't make us glad. But we'll always take a chance, I think, at being rich and sad.

There is nothing so disastrous as a rational investment policy in an irrational world.

John Maynard Keynes

priced and highest yielding of the ten highest-yielding stocks, stand pat. If, on the other hand, some of the stocks have moved up in price and out of the Dow five, kick them out, no matter how much you love them. Sell them and put in new arrivals.

The beauty of the theory is that you don't have to pick the five stocks yourself. It's an automatic system. Emotions don't get in the way. The results have been spectacular. From 1973 to 1995, a $10,000 investment in the Dow Five would have appreciated beyond $1 million. If the same $10,000 had gone into the 30 Dow Jones Industrials, it would have grown to just $208,000. So you are doing five times as well with the Dow Five.

MAHR: It sounds too good to be true.

WESTHEIMER: I can't guarantee that the increase will be the same every year. We check every three or four years and results have been very strong, more than 20.9 percent per year on average.

MAHR: Thank you, Westy. At 89, you're amazing.

WESTHEIMER: And I hope to be here a long time doing what I've always enjoyed – answering money and investment questions.

On August 31, 2005, just a few weeks after our final interview, Julius Westheimer died unexpectedly. He had undergone surgery two weeks earlier for an abdominal obstruction and appeared to be recovering well. Julius was planning to visit the studio of WYPR-FM the next day to tape segments for his daily commentaries on public radio.

"Westy was a legend in the investment business," said Bill Miller, chief executive of Legg Mason Capital Management. "He gave of himself to the local community in a way very few others in the investment community did."

Go to professionals, diversify (remember Enron?), stick to quality, invest for the long pull, don't let every headline throw you off course and don't "time" the market. The time to invest money is when you have it.

Julius Westheimer

How to live on a shoestring.

If you can forgo ambiance, a nice climate, personal safety, good hospitals, job opportunity, accessibility to family and friends, sports and decent restaurants, here are several excellent suggestions to help you live on a shoestring.

1 *Be a tire tramp.* Buy a cheap RV, and get a permit from the Bureau of Land Management. You'll have to keep the campsites tidy and not damage the environment. Also get a solar-powered generator, and it's wise to locate near a water source.

A 20-foot RV for couples has all the amenities anyone can want to make them happy. Camp on a pristine beach in southern Baja, swim nude in the clear, cool, emerald-jade water. Catch fresh fish and barbecue them over a driftwood fire.

2 *Be a squatter.* Find land no one is using. If you live on it seven years without anyone objecting, you can claim it as your own.

"Fran, why don't we sell our Florida apartment? We would save condo fees, taxes and hurricane assessments. We'd buy a cheap, used RV, go out west and live in the desert."

"Are you insane?" she said. "My dermatologist told me to avoid the sun. And you know I'm a Pisces; I love being near the water."

"But, honey, we could reduce our food expenses. For example, coffee. You roast half a pound of barley in the oven. Then grind it with a pound of coffee beans. With coffee at 5 to 8 dollars a pound and barley at 10 cents a pound, we've cut the cost of our coffee in half."

"Let's tow the trailer to a new state and make a fresh start."

"Leave me alone," Fran said.

"And, we would grow our own food," I continued. "I read where you can use a plastic container, like an old water jug, buy a small bag of potting soil and a couple of starter tomato plants. Then you cut the top off the container, fill it with potting soil and plant the tomatoes. We put the tomato plants in a sunny spot in our desert garden and just watch them sprout up."

"IN THE DESERT!" Fran screamed. "Where would I shop? Where would I get my hair and nails done? Who would I talk to? It's a stupid idea."

"Honey, we will enjoy the beautiful sunsets and maybe do a little prospecting in our very own abandoned mine shaft. Think of all the fun we are going to have, my love, and all the money we will save. Why are you smiling, Fran?

"Maybe it is a good idea. If we move near Reno, Nevada, I could gamble all day, get an uncontested divorce for $1,200 and pay for it with your credit card."

"Huh?"

8 Ease someone else's heartache and forget your own.

*It is one of the beautiful compensations of this life that
no man can try to help another without helping himself.*
Ralph Waldo Emerson

Volunteering – a rewarding way to make a difference.
At a time of their lives when many retirees feel bored,
depressed or alienated, volunteer work can be a powerful
antidote. Volunteering provides what most retirees need:
structure, purpose, affiliation, growth and meaning.

"Ninety-five percent of volunteers show a decrease
in chronic pain and an increase in optimism," report
Mary Helen and Shuford Smith in *101 Secrets for a Great
Retirement.* "A study of 2,700 retired men over a ten-year
period revealed that volunteers had a death rate two and a
half times lower than non-volunteers."

*There is no exercise better
for the heart than reaching
down and lifting people up.*
John Andrew Holmer

*If you're bored and depressed with life – my good man,
I'll tell you a wonderful trick,
That will bring you contentment– like nothing else can,
Do something for somebody, quick!*
Unknown

Tel Megiddo is one of the most important archaeological
mounds in Israel. Excavations have uncovered the ruins
of 25 cities dating from 4,000 to 400 B.C.E. Ruined

We make a living by what we get, we make a life by what we give.

Winston Churchill

structures, now visible, belong to the fortified "chariot city," built by King Solomon in the 10th century B.C.E. This biblical city was on the ancient road from Egypt to Syria and Mesopotamia. Found among the ruins were these ancient, prophetic words translated from Hebrew.

A man's real worth is determined by what he does when he has nothing to do.

Volunteer opportunities.

Find an opportunity that fits your interests, skills and schedule. There are hundreds of ways to help out. It's never been easier to find a rewarding way to give back and make a difference.

VolunteerMatch is a leader in the nonprofit world dedicated to helping everyone find a great place to volunteer. Their popular service has become the preferred Internet recruiting tool for more than 30,000 nonprofit organizations. Telephone **415-241-6868** or on the web: **www.VolunteerMatch.org.**

The smallest good deed is better than the grandest good intention.

Duguet

Do you want to volunteer? Try:

* Volunteering for crime prevention
* Teaching, coaching, or mentoring
* Assisting in the political process
* Joining the fight against drunk driving
* Helping feed the hungry, homeless and elderly
* Working in a hospital or hospice
* Spending some of your time protecting the earth
* Sharing your unique talents, interest, and experience

* Having an overseas adventure
* Volunteering your pet

1 Volunteer for crime prevention.
My wife Fran wanted to participate in the field of crime prevention. She volunteered for service with the state attorney's office in Fort Pierce, Florida.

After taking a five-week training course, Fran was assigned to the spousal abuse section, manning a telephone hotline. Her duties were clearly outlined in writing.

> "When a call comes in, the victim-abuse operator is to record accurately the information. At all times the operator is to project to the caller a calm, objective demeanor, and above all, express no emotion or opinion as to the merits of the alleged victim's claims. Then immediately report the caller's information to the appropriate authority."

To the world you may be one person, but to one person you may be the world.

Anonymous

On Fran's second night of duty, a distress call came in on the spousal abuse hotline. A hysterical young woman described in vivid detail how her husband had beaten her.

"HE DID WHAT?" Fran screamed. "Don't worry, dear," she told the alleged victim, "we'll fix that SON-OF-A-BITCH!" After hurried consultation, a few days later, the state attorney's office reassigned Fran to the filing division.

2 Teaching, coaching, or mentoring.
There are many ways to help adults and children in your local school system by tutoring, substitute teaching, coaching or mentoring young people in need.

"My name is Mr. Collins. I'll be teaching you English literature, and I'm armed."

> *I wondered why somebody didn't do something. Then I realized, I am somebody.*
> Anonymous

Contact your local school system or call:

* Big Brothers/Big Sisters of America **215-567-7000**
* Literacy Volunteers of America **315-445-8000**
* Help One Student to Succeed (HOSTS) **800-833-4678**
* American Library Association **800-545-2433**

3 Assist in the political process.
No matter what your political-party preference is, if you
want an uplifting civic adventure, volunteer at your local

political party headquarters. There is always a need for volunteers to man phones, do door-to-door solicitation, hold signs at polling places, and drive elderly people to vote.

During the last presidential election, I volunteered. In an old Florida storefront that served as the Democratic Party's temporary headquarters, I located the person in charge, Vera, an in-your-face young black lady from Washington, D.C.

I said, "I've been an Army officer, a corporate executive, a writer and lecturer on advertising. What can I do to help?"

"You got a car?" asked Vera.

"Yes."

"You're a driver. Be here at 7 tomorrow, sharp."

I arrived on a steamy-hot election day, thinking about the elderly, poor, and disabled people I would be driving to vote.

"DRIVER," Vera bellowed, pointing at me. "Go up to the Fort Pierce office, pick up placards and water. MOVE IT!"

When I returned with my cargo, Vera saw me. "DRIVER," she yelled. "Go pick up the foot-long subs we ordered, divvy them up and deliver them, with the water, to our poll-watchers."

"But don't I get to drive any – "

"And don't take all day," Vera added.

At 5 o'clock I left and joined Fran at the office of the Supervisor of Elections, where we counted absentee ballots long into the evening.

If you want happiness for an hour, take a nap. If you want happiness for a day, go fishing. If you want happiness for a month, get married. If you want happiness for a year, inherit a fortune. If you want happiness for a lifetime – help someone else.

Chinese proverb

There are times when I become disenchanted with politics and politicians. But when you assist in the political process and join with volunteers of all ages and stripes who just show up and ask unselfishly, "What can I do to help?" it rekindles a respect for the American citizenry. I'm really going to miss Vera.

4 Join the fight against drunk driving.

The founding of the organization Mothers Against Drunk Driving (MADD) is an example of how volunteering brings out the best in an individual. In 1980, thirteen-year-old Cari Lightner was walking to a church activity when she was struck and killed by a drunk driver. At the time her grief-stricken mother, Candy Lightner, was not even registered to vote. Ms. Lightner put her grief into action and started Mothers Against Drunk Driving.

Today, there are over 300 chapters of MADD, which have altered public opinion about drunk driving. **Call 800-Get-MADD.**

5 Help feed the hungry, homeless and elderly.

According to the U.S. Conference of Mayors, even before Hurricane Katrina in 2005, there were an estimated three million homeless people in the United States.

It's a memorable life experience to take your family to a homeless shelter to prepare food, to interact with fellow volunteers, and to serve our fellow human beings down on their luck. Fran and I have volunteered at the Helping Hand Shelter in Baltimore, serving Thanksgiving and Christmas dinners.

I do get paid for my voluntary work. I just don't get paid money.

Unknown volunteer

To help feed the hungry, contact:

* International Union of Gospel Missions
  800-624-5156
* Second Harvest **800-532-FOOD**
* Meals-on-Wheels
  (In phone book under aging services).
* Mazon **310-442-0030**

6 Work in a hospital or hospice.

Hospice is a new concept in America. In 1976, Father Paul von Lobkowit, age sixty-four, started the Hospice of St. John in Lakewood, Colorado, with only "ten cents and a can of paint." The hospice serves terminally ill patients. There are over 2,500 hospices in the United States with over 90 percent of the care being provided in the patient's home. Volunteers are trained to offer respite care for the family as well as support to the patient.

Many tasks are available for hospital volunteers that will provide a meaningful experience for you and for the people whose thanks you will earn.

Unless someone like you cares a whole, awful lot, things aren't going to get better, they're NOT!

Dr. Seuss, *The Lorax*

> *Thanks for all the little things*
> *The "done-and-then-forgotten" things,*
> *The "oh-it's-simply-nothing" things*
> *That make our days much brighter.*
> *The unobtrusive, friendly things,*
> *And "never-mind-the-trouble" things,*
> *And "won't-you-let-me-help-you" things,*
> *You've made our hearts much lighter.*
>
> Author unknown

7 Spend some of your time protecting the earth.
Global warming is one of the most serious challenges facing
us today. To protect the health and economic well-being
of current and future generations, we must reduce our
emissions of heat-trapping gases by using the technology,
know-how, and practical solutions already at our disposal.

*Only when the last tree has died
and the last river been poisoned
and the last fish been caught will
we realize we cannot eat money.*

Cree Indian proverb

*"Call this an iceberg? When I was a kid we
wouldn't have called this an iceberg!"*

To help protect the earth, contact:

A volunteer is a person who believes that people can make a difference – and is willing to prove it.

Anonymous

Greenpeace: Greenpeace is the leading independent organization using nonviolent direct action and communication to expose global environmental problems and to promote solutions essential to a green and peaceful future. **www.greenpeace.org**

National Audubon Society: Audubon's mission is to conserve and restore natural ecosystems, focusing on birds, other wildlife, and their habitats for the benefit of humanity and the earth's biological diversity. **www.audubon.org**

Sierra Club: The Sierra Club is America's oldest and largest grassroots environmental organization. **www.sierraclub.org**

Teach us love, compassion, and honor that we may heal the earth and heal each other.

Ojibwa prayer

WWF: Known worldwide by its panda logo, World Wildlife Fund (WWF) leads international efforts to protect endangered species and their habitats. Now in its fifth decade, WWF works in more than 100 countries around the globe to conserve the diversity of life on earth. With nearly 1.2 million members in the U.S. and another 4 million worldwide, WWF is the world's largest privately financed conservation organization. **www.worldwildlife.org**

8 Share your unique talents, interests, and experience.
Our friends Elaine and Lolly are docents at art museums. They demonstrate that volunteers are unpaid not because

they are worthless, but because they are priceless. Contact your local museum or call the American Association for Museum Volunteers, **202-289-6575.**

With cutbacks in federal funding for public television and radio, volunteer efforts are needed. Fran is a former member of American Federation of Television and Radio Artists (AFTRA). As a volunteer, she records books and reads newspapers for the blind. The National Library Service for the Blind and Physically Handicapped also produces books and magazines in Braille.

Millions of seniors are unable to read. Call your local station or National Friends of Public Broadcasting **317-636-2020 or (NPR) 202-414-2000.**

Everybody can be great...
because anybody can serve.
You don't have to have a
college degree to serve. You
don't have to make your
subject and your verb agree
to serve. You only need a
heart full of grace. A soul
generated by love.

Martin Luther King, Jr.

Imagine what a harmonious world it would be if every
single person shared a little of what he is good at doing.

Quincy Jones

Habitat for Humanity International is a nonprofit, ecumenical Christian housing ministry. HFHI seeks to eliminate poverty housing and homelessness from the world, and to make decent shelter a matter of conscience and action.

Habitat invites people of all backgrounds, races and religions to build houses together in partnership with families in need. Habitat has built more than 200,000 houses around the world, providing more than 1,000,000 people in more than 3,000 communities with safe, decent, affordable shelter. **229-924-6935**

9 Volunteer your pet.

Pet Partners is a service program of Delta Society. Pet Partner teams include dogs, cats, birds, and other domesticated animals who, with their owners, visit nursing homes, hospitals, schools, treatment centers and other facilities. These human-animal teams share their love and time with people who need it most, and make a surprising difference. **425-226-7157**

How wonderful it is that nobody need wait a single moment before starting to improve the world.

Anne Frank

10 Have an overseas adventure.

Volunteering overseas can be a rewarding and enriching life experience. The following organizations offer programs for seniors.

Amizade. Provides community service, intercultural exploration and understanding through community-driven volunteer programs. **888-973-4443**

American Jewish World Service. Providing nonsectarian humanitarian assistance and relief to disadvantaged people worldwide. Last year AJWS sent over 300 volunteers to the developing world offering grants, technical assistance, and emergency relief. **800-889-7146**

Catholic Medical Missions Board. CMMB is the leading U.S.-based Catholic charity focusing on global health care, particularly the well-being of women and children. CMMB works to fight HIV/AIDS from Africa to Asia, to combat tuberculosis in Zambia, and to provide primary health care in Latin America and the Caribbean. **800-678-5659**

Global Volunteers. For more than 20 years, Global Volunteers has mobilized short-term international volunteers for service and work programs on six continents. You can choose by region of the world or by project. Service projects include child care, teaching English, health care, conservation work, construction repair, and more. No specialized skills needed. **800-487-1074**

The pleasure of doing good is the only one that will not wear out.

Chinese proverb

I shall pass through this world but once. Any good therefore that I can do or any kindness that I can show to any human being, let me do it now. Let me not defer or neglect it for I shall not pass this way again.

Mahatma Gandhi

9

Demonstrate your faith by example – not just words.

This is my simple religion. There is no need for temples; no need for complicated philosophy. Our own brain, our own heart is the temple; the philosophy is kindness.

Dalai Lama

"Of course I hope to find gold. But my real goal is spiritual growth and inner peace."

Spiritual growth & inner peace.

Spirituality concerns our personal search to find greater meaning and purpose in existence. The word "spiritual" derives from the French word *esprit* and refers to the breath or breathing. When you are filled with spiritual energy, you are inspired.

Spirituality and religion are different aspects of human experience. Spirituality has been called the mystical face of religion.

A flowering of spirituality.

Spirituality is lived out in the way that we show love, kindness, care, and compassion to others.

> *Three things in human life are important.*
> *The first is to be kind. The second is to be kind.*
> *And the third is to be kind.*
> Henry James

A major poll commissioned by *Newsweek* magazine and Beliefnet.com reveals that nearly two of every three Americans polled described themselves as religious. But an even larger number – four out of five – described themselves as "spiritual."

"A flowering of spirituality was everywhere we looked," the *Newsweek* article said. "In the hollering, swooning, foot-stomping services of the new wave of Pentecostals; in Catholic churches where worshipers passed the small hours of the night alone contemplating the

My therapist told me the way to achieve true inner peace is to finish what I start. So for today, I have finished 2 bags of M&M's and a chocolate cake. I feel better already.

Dave Barry

Eucharist, and among Jews seeking God in the mystical thickets of Kabbalah. Also in the efforts of American Muslims to achieve a more God-centered Islam."

Access your spirituality.
It used to be such a simple question to answer. But now you might be "spiritual but not religious" – or raised in one faith but practicing another. Maybe you're a Methodist but think of yourself more as an evangelical, or a seeker who is anti-religion – or born again.

The spiritual life does not remove us from the world but leads us deeper into it.
Henri J. M. Nouwan
Dutch Catholic Priest

You may be interested in a twenty-question multiple choice quiz sponsored by the web site Beliefnet. Here is one sample question from the quiz "What's your spiritual type?"

Question: I believe that God:

___1 Exists and intervenes in daily events.

___2 Exists but does not intervene in daily events.

___3 Is a spiritual ideal, not an actual being.

___4 Does not exist.

This free and graded quiz on **www.beliefnet.com** is offered to help you learn more about your spiritual self.

Yoga – a spiritual practice for the body.
Of the spiritual practices for the body, mind, and spirit, the most popular is yoga, an ancient system of exercises originating in India.   Yoga is not a passing fad, but a genuine cultural phenomenon.

Zen question:
If a man is in the forest talking to himself, with no one present, is he still wrong?

Anonymous

"The Master Ramachandra is on vacation. Concentrate on your breathing, meditate, pay your dues. This is a recording."

Namaste

*"Namaste...*The divine in me bows to the divine in you," said Yoga instructor Sara Ramakrishma—nee Sarah Rothstein-- at the spa in Pompano Beach, Florida.

Fran and I had put on too much weight. Our friends, Myles and Bev, recommended the Pompano spa where they had each lost eight pounds. This week was a Father's Day special; husbands were invited free. I was the only man in the yoga class.

Ms. Ramakrishma lit a candle, lowered the lights and pressed the start button on her tape recorder. The track was called *Temple Garden*, played on a *shakuhachi*, a Japanese bamboo flute. The music set the mood for our spiritual journey.

Yoga is a word meaning *union,* and as the instructor explained, "Our goal is to approach what the Buddha called 'Oneness with the Universe.'

"Meditation," intoned Sara, "is mindfulness. To breathe in and out consciously—to touch each breath with our mind. When you practice this way, your mind and body come into alignment. Your wandering thoughts come to a stop. Peace is near."

My ass hurt; I have a coccyx bone problem. The floor was hard as a rock. I wanted a pillow to sit on, but was afraid to ask.

"Breathe in," the instructor continued. "We calm our bodies—like drinking a glass of cool water. Feel the freshness permeate your being. Your mind and body become one.

My son has taken up meditation. At least it's better than sitting around and doing nothing.

Max Kaufman

Breathe out and smile. One smile can relax hundreds of muscles in your face. When you see an image of the Buddha, he is always smiling."

I breathed deeply, allowing my fears about never finding a publisher for my book to gently recede. I listened to the languid music, breathing in and breathing out. A calm, peaceful feeling settled over my mind and body.

Sara said, "We are now going to get into the *Sarvangasana*, or as we call it, the 'shoulder-stand' position. Please lie flat on your back and inhale through your nostrils. Now place your palms face-down on the floor. Pressing down, lift your torso from the waist up off the floor, arching the spine backwards and straightening the arms. Keep the hips on the floor—"

"Excuse me, Miss Ramakrishma," I said. "I have osteoarthritis. Do I have to do this exercise?"

"The Buddha says, 'Life is suffering,' she replied.

I tried to refocus on the candle and the music in an unsuccessful effort to ignore the gnawing pain in my back and find inner peace. I also had to urinate. My overflowing kidneys were interfering with my reaching that perfect state of calmness.

As I picked up my towel and headed for the exit, I smiled at the ladies in the yoga class, bowed to Sara Ramakrishma and said, "Namaste."

"Men are such wimps," I heard someone mumble.

"Did you hear about the Buddhist who refused his dentist's Novocain during root canal work?"

"He wanted to transcend dental medication."

My *sole literary ambition is
to write one good novel, then
retire to my hut in the desert,
assume the lotus position,
compose my mind and senses,
and sink into meditation,
comtemplating my novel.*
Edward Abbey

*"If I knew the meaning of life, would I be
sitting in a cave in my underpants?"*

Meditation.

Meditation is an easy-to-learn technique to enable you to
alleviate stress, relax, and gain precious insights and peace of
mind.

At the Pompano spa, in addition to yoga, I learned
about meditation. Here's more or less how it works.

Step 1: Find a spot to sit quietly, and undisturbed.

RRRRRRRRIIINNNNG!

"Mac, get the phone," Fran said. "I'm reading the papers."

"I'm trying to meditate, Fran. YOU get the phone."

"How am I supposed to know you're meditating?" she replied. "Excuse me for living."

Her karma ran over my dogma.

Anonymous

Step 2: Concentrate on breathing. Breathe deeply and exhale slowly, letting your body relax.

I focus my mind on a *mantra* – a word or syllable to exclude intruding thoughts that crowd into my head – like the attractive, dark-haired, Cuban beauty, Carmen, next door.

My mantra is *Om*. It creates a sound vibration leading to a higher awareness. *Om*...I feel my breath entering through the top of my head and washing down to my toes. I'm at peace.

"Is it OK if I run the dishwasher?" yells Fran.
I don't answer. *"Om...Om."*

Step 3: Tensing muscle groups. Starting with your toes, tense tightly for a count of twenty. Relax and take deep breaths. Tighten the leg muscles. Sometimes the tightening gives me leg cramps.

"I hear you walking around," Fran says. "While you're up help me make the bed."

"No. I have a terrible cramp in my leg. I'm walking it off."

Meditation is the tongue of the soul and the language of our spirit.
    Jeremy Taylor

Return to a comfortable position and continue to tighten muscle groups: buttocks, abdomen, shoulders and neck muscles.

RRRRRRRRIIINNNNNG!

"I can't talk now, Susan," Fran stage-whispers into the phone. "His royal highness is meditating."

Step 4: Think of a peaceful place. A sandy beach with ocean waves gently lapping on the shore. Through meditation, I developed the self-discipline to treat my body as a temple and the willpower to avoid eating fattening, starchy foods.

RRRRRRRRIIINNNNNG!

"I'll get it," Fran says. "It's Martine and John. They want us to go to the new all-you-can-eat Italian buffet in Little Italy."

"Sounds great!"

Religion.

Religion should be a remedy to help reduce the conflict and the suffering in the world, and not another source of conflict.

The Rev. Canon Renée Miller says, "When you think of being spiritual rather than religious, you will naturally be led to embrace a practice of piety. Religious piety does not have to be a straightjacket. There is an immense amount of freedom in how you give voice and substance to the spiritual longing you feel."

As examples, Rev. Miller suggests that piety can involve simple silence and centering. Or perhaps it will be lived out in the way that people show care and compassion to others. Or articulated through prayer and surrendering oneself to God. Rev. Miller adds that piety can be manifested through embracing such virtues as patience, kindness, truthfulness, or unconditional love.

Humility.

Humility is the state of being humble. A humble person is supposed to be unpretentious and modest: someone who does not think that he or she is better or more important than others. In monotheistic religions, humility can be seen as a form of respect towards and acknowledgment of a supreme being.

To know a person's religion we need not listen to his profession of faith but must find his brand of intolerance.
Eric Hoffer

> One day a rabbi and his cantor walked into their synagogue together and found themselves overwhelmed in God's presence. Both fell to the ground in humility and awe. They exclaimed in unison, "O Lord, I am nothing!"

The synagogue janitor was cleaning behind one of the pillars when he saw these two devout men fall to their knees. Moved by their display of devotion and humility, he too fell to the ground and cried, "O Lord, I am nothing!"

The cantor nudged the rabbi and whispered, "Hey, look who thinks he's nothing!"

A good example is the best sermon.

Anonymous

Prayer.

The only time my prayers are never answered is on the golf course.

Billy Graham

Prayer is an effort to communicate with God, or to some deity or deities, or spiritual entity, either to offer praise, to make a request, or simply to express one's thoughts or emotions. We should not pray to ask for something that is within our power to do, and we should demonstrate our faith by example – not just words.

Listen

We cannot merely pray to You, O God, to end war,
For we know that You have made the world in a way
That man must find his own path to peace
Within himself and with his neighbor.
We cannot merely pray to You, O God, to end starvation;
For you have already given us the resources
With which to feed the entire world
If we would only use them wisely.
We cannot merely pray to You, O God,
To root out prejudice,

For You have already given us eyes
With which to see the good in all men
If we would only use them rightly.
We cannot merely pray to You, O God, to end despair,
For You have already given us the power
To clear away slums and to give hope
If only we would use our power justly.
We cannot merely pray to You, O God, to end disease,
For You have already given us great minds with which
To search out cures and healing,
If only we could use them constructively.
Therefore we pray to You instead, O God,
For strength, determination, and willpower,
To do instead of just to pray,
To become instead of merely to wish.

Jack Riemer, *Likrat Shabbit*

Prayer indeed is good, but while calling on the gods a man should himself lend a hand.

Hippocrates

Comparative religion quiz.

Match the following listed faith or group with the questions below: *Baptist; Buddhist; Agnostic; Atheist; Catholic; New Age; Jewish.*

1 The leader of what faith or group said to God, "Let me see if I have it right, the Arabs get the oil and we get the right to cut off the tips of our what?" _____

2 The member of what faith or group said, "Somebody burned a question mark on my front lawn." _____

"Do you know what you get when you cross a Jehovah's Witness with an atheist?"

"Someone who knocks at your door for no apparent reason."

3 The member of what faith or group said, "I believe in spirit guides and an afterlife, so I'm taking a change of underwear." _____

4 The leader of what faith or group said to the hot dog vendor, "Make me one with everything." _____

5 What faith or group has the basic theology that if you hold people under water long enough, they'll eventually come around to your way of thinking? _____

6 What group is a non-prophet organization? _____

7 A member of what faith or group gives up sex for life, and once a week people come in and tell him all the highlights of theirs? _____

Answers:
1 Jewish; 2 Agnostic; 3 New Age; 4 Buddhist; 5 Baptist; 6 Atheist; 7 Catholic.

10

Laugh. Life's too short to be anything – but happy.

The time to be happy is now.
The key to being happy is to make others so.

Anonymous

He who laughs, lasts.
According to the Bible, "A merry heart doeth good like a medicine." Now, modern science is validating King Solomon's Old Testament proverb. While we've done away with leeches, the ancient idea that "humor heals" has become more widely accepted.

There ain't much fun in medicine, but there's a heck of a lot of medicine in fun.

Josh Billings

"It's nice to see he hasn't lost his sense of humor."

Laughing is good medicine.

"Laughing is good for your health," says Michael Miller, MD, director of preventive cardiology at the University of Maryland Medical Center in Baltimore.

Miller and his colleagues believe that laughter causes the body to release natural chemicals known as endorphins – pleasure-producing agents best known for producing the "runner's high" – that may counteract the effects of stress hormones and cause blood vessels to dilate. Several hospitals across the country with oncology wards are developing humor programs for their patients.

Laughter is the best medicine, but in certain situations the Heimlich maneuver may be more appropriate.

Anonymous

I live by this credo: Have a little laugh at life and look around you for happiness instead of sadness. Laughter has always brought me out of unhappy situations. Even in your darkest moment, you usually can find something to laugh about if you try hard enough.

Red Skelton

Norman Cousins

One of the pioneers in linking laughter to healing was Norman Cousins, the editor of the *Saturday Review* for over forty years. In 1960 he was stricken with a crippling, life-threatening disease, ankylosing spondylitis. Cousins was told that his chances for survival were one in five hundred and that he had little time to live.

Norman Cousins assumed responsibility for his own healing. He designed a regimen of high doses of vitamin C and positive emotions, including daily doses of laughter with Marx Brothers movies and *Candid Camera* reruns. And it worked.

Laughter is inner jogging.
Norman Cousins

Cousins chronicled his recovery in *Anatomy of an Illness*, describing how he used laughter to facilitate his recuperation. He said, "Laughter serves as a blocking agent. Like a bulletproof vest, it may help protect you against the ravages of negative emotions that can assault you in disease."

On one occasion, I was seated next to Norman Cousins at a World Federalist dinner that my wife, Fran, was co-chairing. I was unaware Cousins was the honoree. He sat down next to me, shook my hand, and said, "Hello, I'm Norman Cousins."

"Hi, Norm," I replied. "I'm Mac, what do you do?"

Norman Cousins smiled politely.

"I can't take you anywhere," Fran hissed.

Later in the evening, Mr. Cousins concluded his speech by saying, "Extensive experiments have been conducted, working with a significant number of human beings, showing that laughter contributes to good health."

Over a dozen studies have now documented that humor does have the power to reduce pain in many patients – scientific evidence to buttress Norman Cousin's intuition.

The world's funniest joke.

A few years ago, a British research group at the University of Hertfordshire set out to discover the world's funniest joke. More than 300,000 people from around the world visited an Internet website called laughlab where they submitted 40,000 jokes and rated other people's submissions. Here is the top rated joke.

Two hunters are out in the woods when one of them collapses. He doesn't seem to be breathing and his eyes are glazed. The other guy takes out his cell phone and calls the emergency services.

He gasps: "My friend is dead! What can I do?"

The operator says: "Calm down, I can help. First, let's make sure he's dead."

There is a silence, then a gunshot is heard.

Back on the phone, the guy says: "OK, now what?"

Humor releases repressed thoughts of sex and death.
Sigmund Freud, in his study of laughter, described the release/relief theory, explaining that laughter is a physical manifestation of repressed thoughts of taboos such as sex and death – perhaps explaining the popularity of mortality and sexual humor.

Sexual Humor: A Frenchman and an Italian were hunting pheasant. Suddenly, a beautiful nude girl ran by. The Frenchman said, "I'd love some of that." So the Italian shot her.

Mortality Humor: A woman is upset at her husband's funeral. "You have him in a brown suit and I wanted him in a blue suit." The mortician says, "We'll take care of it, ma'am," and yells back, "Ed, switch the heads on two and four!"

Different types of humor.
Pun: A pun is a word that has more than one meaning, depending on the context. Humor occurs when the context is changed to give the word an alternative meaning.

Women claim that what they look for in a man is a sense of humor, but I don't believe it. Who do you want removing your bra--Brad Pitt or the Three Stooges?

Bruce Smirnoff

A boy asks his father to make a noise like a frog. When the father asks why, he says, "Because mom said we could go to Disneyland after you croaked."

Hello, this is the Incontinence Hotline. Can you hold, please?
Anonymous

Exaggeration: Many comedians use exaggeration to add humor to commonplace examples.

Chris Rock says, "We don't need no gun control, we need bullet control. Bullets should cost five thousand dollars, then people would think before they killed somebody.

" 'Man, I would blow your head off if I could afford it. I'm going to get me another job, save my money. You better hope I can't get no bullets on layaway.' "

Surprise: Humor based on the element of surprise:

A woman got on a bus holding a baby. The bus driver said: "That's the ugliest baby I've ever seen." In a huff, the woman slammed her fare into the fare box and took an aisle seat near the rear of the bus.

The man seated next to her sensed that she was agitated and asked her what was wrong. "The bus driver insulted me," she fumed.

The man sympathized and said: "Why, he's a public servant and shouldn't say things to insult passengers."

"You're right," she said. "I think I'll go back up there and give him a piece of my mind."

"Good idea," the man said. "Here, let me hold your monkey."

We do have a zeal for laughter in most situations, give or take a dentist.
Joseph Heller

The Put-Down. The put-down is usually used to insult other people for a laugh. Rodney Dangerfield derived his humor by putting down himself instead of other people.

> "My psychiatrist told me I'm going crazy," Rodney Dangerfield said. "I told him, 'If you don't mind, I'd like a second opinion.' He said, 'All right. You're ugly too!'"

I laughed all the way to the ureteroscopy.
A sense of humor can help you tolerate the unpleasant, and cope with the unexpected, but doesn't do much for kidney stone pain. A few years ago, I had a kidney stone attack. X-rays confirmed that the large 7 mm stone required removal by a ureteroscopy operation using a special fiber optic telescope stuck up my "you-know-what" and passed through the urinary tract to the ureter. The stone was smashed into tiny pieces with a laser. Then they inserted a catheter and sent me home.

To succeed in life, you need three things: a wishbone, a backbone and a funny bone.

Reba McEntire

The next day I returned to Johns Hopkins Bayview (a teaching hospital) for the catheter removal. A large, no-nonsense, African American nurse with two cute student nurses in tow said, "Take off your pants and underwear, and hop up on the table."

When you are in pain and discomfort, modesty is irrelevant. The honcho nurse gently lifted my penis, demonstrating to her giggling students how to remove my uncomfortable catheter tube – giving each one a chance to participate. I said, "I've never had three different women handling my penis at one time before."

"In your dreams, Sugar," the nurse said. "Let's go, girls."

Learn a joke.

You can do it. Here's an easy one. Tell it today. Two cannibals are eating a clown. One cannibal turns to the other and asks, "This taste funny to you?"

A man without humor is like a car without shock absorbers.

Anonymous

Give me a healthy body, Lord,
*   and sense to keep it at its best.*
Give me clarity of mind, good Lord,
*   with learning as my quest.*
Give me a sense of humor, Lord,
*   and the grace to see a joke,*
To get some happiness from life,
*   and pass it on to other folk.*

Unknown

What's happiness?

The pursuit of happiness is described in the Declaration of Independence as a right of all Americans, but the Constitution only guarantees the right to pursue this elusive state – you have to catch it yourself.

What's the use of happiness? It can't buy you money.

Henny Youngman

If you observe a happy man, you will find him building a boat, writing a symphony, growing double dahlias, or looking for dinosaur eggs in the Gobi desert. He will have become aware that he is happy in the course of living life twenty-four crowded hours of each day.

W. Beran Wolfe

The Happiness Formula: H = S + C + V

"More words have been penned about defining this promiscuously overused word, *happiness,* than about almost any philosophical question," says Dr. Martin Seligman, the father of the positive psychology movement, a professor of psychology at the University of Pennsylvania and author of *Authentic Happiness.* Seligman offers the following Happiness Formula: H (enduring happiness) = S (your genetic set point for happiness) + C (circumstances) + V (variables).

H = Enduring happiness.

Enduring happiness comes from volunteer activities like crime prevention; teaching, coaching or mentoring children; helping to house and feed the homeless; raising funds to improve health and find cures for disease; working in a hospital; beautifying the community and protecting the environment.

S = Your genetic set point for happiness.

Richard Lucas, a professor at Michigan State University, describes a happiness set point that is ingrained in us to which we migrate back to after extreme positive and negative life experiences.

Happiness is determined more by one's state of mind than by external events. Researchers surveying Illinois lottery winners and British pool winners found that the initial high eventually wore off and winners returned to their usual set point of happiness.

If you can't be happy where you are, it's a cinch you can't be happy where you ain't.

Charles "Tremendous" Jones

C = Circumstances: money, marriage, religion.

Money. In America, real income has doubled since 1960. Yet our divorce rate has also doubled, teen suicide has tripled and depression has increased tenfold.

Dr. Tedd Mitchell, in *USA Weekend,* explains that our culture bombards us with images of what we think should make us happy. Get rich! Get skinny! Get popular!

They say a person needs three things to be happy in this world. Someone to love, something to do, and something to hope for.

Tom Bodett

"I could cry when I think of the years I wasted accumulating money, only to learn that my cheerful disposition is genetic."

People who buy into this way of thinking are setting themselves up for disappointment. Developing daily habits that involve enjoyable work and meaningful connections to others leads to the very important sense of self-worth.

Marriage. The National Opinion Research Center surveyed 35,000 Americans over the last thirty years; 40 percent of married people said they were "very happy," compared to only 24 percent of the unmarried, divorced, separated, and widowed people. Another survey found that if you marry someone who doesn't appreciate you, tries to control you, and always has to be right, you may be unhappy. They also discovered that going without water for long periods of time makes you thirsty.

I've been married for 56 years. I was single for 25 years, and I just got sick and tired of finishing my own sentences.

Religion. If for no other reason, religious affiliation provides both a social support and community participation, which are happiness derivatives. Notwithstanding the happiness spread by the Inquisition, the Crusades and all the bloody wars fought over religion, I can still connect the dots between religion and happiness.

I am fundamentally a religious person, and consider the belief in God to be the basic source of moral values. I know from personal experience in Korea that there is truth in the quote, "There are no atheists in foxholes."

I don't agree with a few evangelists and all insurance companies who refer to hurricanes, earthquakes, tsunamis, and other natural disasters as "acts of God." I prefer Rabbi Harold S. Kushner's concept that hurricanes, earthquakes,

Thousands of candles can be lighted from a single candle, and the life of the candle will not be shortened. Happiness never decreases by being shared.

Buddha

and their like are acts of nature; that nature is morally blind, and that we don't hold God responsible for all the unfair things that happen in the world.

"The God I believe in," says Kushner, "does not send us the problems. He gives us the strength to cope with the problems."

V = Variable factors: gratification and pleasure.
The two factors which you can control are pleasure and gratification. Gratification is achieved by doing something worthwhile.

Albert Schweitzer said, "I don't know what your destiny will be, but one thing I do know: the only ones among you who will be really happy are those who have sought and found how to serve."

Unlike gratification, pleasures are processed through our five senses of taste, smell, sight, sound, and touch. Pleasures are momentary urges and joys that fade away once the stimuli is gone.

For me, some variable pleasures are the taste of a home-baked blueberry pie with vanilla ice cream; the fragrant smell of fresh-cut roses; the sight of an orange and violet sun rising slowly over the Atlantic; the sound of Ray Bryant on the piano; and the feel of Fran cuddled close in bed on a cold night, or a hot night, or any night. AHHH.

The happiest are those who do the most for others.
Booker T. Washington

"Oh-oh! Look who's back!"

The purpose of life is to seek happiness.
His Holiness, the XIVth Dalai Lama, is a man who lost an
entire country as a result of a brutal invasion; a man who
has lived in exile for four decades while an entire nation
places their hopes and dreams of freedom on him.

*Happiness is when what you
think, what you say, and
what you do are in harmony.*

Mohandas K. Gandhi

The Dalai Lama teaches that the very purpose of our existence is to seek happiness. He said, "The proper utilization of time is this: if you can – serve other people. If not, at least refrain from harming them. That is the basis of my philosophy. For life to be of value, we must develop basic human qualities – warmth, kindness, compassion. Then our life becomes meaningful and more peaceful – happier."

He explained that technical development alone cannot lead to lasting happiness. In the world today, there are societies that are wealthy materially, yet among them are many who are not happy. Just underneath the surface of affluence there is a kind of emotional unrest, leading to frustration, unnecessary quarrels, reliance on drugs or alcohol, and in the worst case, suicide. So there is no guarantee that wealth alone can give you joy or happiness.

Justice is the only worship.
Love is the only priest.
Ignorance is the only slavery.
Happiness is the only good.
The time to be happy is now.
The place to be happy is here.
*The way to be happy is to make
others so.*

Robert Green Ingersoll

Index of Sources

To order more copies of *You're Retired Now. Relax,* as gifts for friends and family members, send $14.95 per book, plus $4.00 for shipping and handling. Free shipping on orders of ten or more copies to one destination. Make your check payable to:

Treasure Coast Press
4828 N. Kings Hwy., #127
Fort Pierce, FL 34951

...also by Malcolm Mahr

What Makes A Marriage Work

"Mac Mahr has put together fifty of the most informative and funny insights about marriage ever to go to press."

John Hamilton Lewis, Author, *Samsara*

To order *What Makes a Marriage Work* send $14.95 per book, plus $4.00 for shipping and handling. Free shipping on orders of ten or more copies to one destination. Make your check payable to:

Treasure Coast Press
4828 N. Kings Hwy., #127 , Fort Pierce, FL 34951

What Makes a Marriage Work is also available on www.barnesandnoble.com, or www.amazon.com